THE ADLERWEG

About the Author

Mike Wells has been walking long-distance footpaths for 25 years, after a holiday in New Zealand gave him the long-distance walking bug. Within a few years he had walked the major British trails, enjoying their range of terrain from straightforward downland tracks through to upland paths and challenging mountain routes. He then ventured into France – walking sections of the Grande Randonnée, including the GR5 through the Alps from Lake Geneva to the Mediterranean – and Italy to explore the Dolomites Alta Via routes. Further afield, he has walked in Poland, Slovakia, Slovenia, Norway and even Chilean Patagonia.

While working for a travel company he made frequent trips to the Austrian Tyrol, getting away whenever he could to walk in the mountains. It was on one of these trips that he first encountered the 'Adlerweg', a project to create a long-distance path stretching across the Tyrol from St Johann to St Anton. Subsequent visits enabled him to walk the entire path a number of times.

THE ADLERWEG

THE EAGLE'S WAY ACROSS THE AUSTRIAN TYROL

by

Mike Wells

2 POLICE SQUARE, MILNTHORPE, CUMBRIA LA7 7PY
www.cicerone.co.uk

© Mike Wells 2012
First edition 2012
ISBN: 978 1 85284 641 1
Printed by KHL Printing, Singapore.
A catalogue record for this book is available from the British Library.
All photographs are by the author unless otherwise stated.

*To Christine, who accompanied me through the Tyrol until stopped by a broken
leg, and Nassereith Bergrettungsdienst, who rescued her from Heimbachtal.*

Front cover: Looking down into Birkkarklamm gorge, with Hinterautal at the end
of the valley and Lafatscher on the skyline (Stage 11)

CONTENTS

Map key 7
Overview map 8

INTRODUCTION 11
Background 13
The Adlerweg 16
National parks and protected areas 17
Preparation 17
Getting there 21
Navigation 24
Maps 27
Accommodation 29
Food and drink 31
Amenities and services 37
The natural environment 39
What to take 43
Safe walking 44
About this guide 48

THE ROUTE
SECTION 1
Kaisergebirge 50
Stage 1   St Johann in Tirol to Gaudeamushutte 50
Stage 2   Gaudeamushutte to Hintersteinersee 57
Stage 3   Hintersteinersee to Kufstein 61

SECTION 2
Brandenberger Alpen and Rofangebirge 66
Stage 4   Langkampfen to Buchackeralm 66
Stage 5   Buchackeralm to Kaiserhaus 73
Stage 6   Kaiserhaus to Steinberg am Rofan 76
Stage 7   Steinberg am Rofan to Mauritzalm 80
Stage U6   Kaiserhaus to Bayreutherhutte 85
Stage U7   Bayreutherhutte to Mauritzalm 89

SECTION 3
Karwendelgebirge 93
Stage 8   Maurach to Lamsenjochhutte 93
Stage 9   Lamsenjochhutte to Falkenhutte 101
Stage 10   Falkenhutte to Karwendelhaus 104
Stage 11   Karwendelhaus to Hallerangerhaus 107

Stage 12   Hallerangerhaus to Hafelekarhaus 111
Stage U9   Lamsenjochhutte to Vomperberg. 115
Stage U10   Vomperberg to Absam 120
Stage U11   Absam to Pfeishutte 124

SECTION 4
Innsbruck and Patscherkofel 128
Stage 12a   Innsbruck city tour 128
Stage 13   Patscherkofelhaus to Tulfeinalm 133
Stage 14   Hochzirl to Solsteinhaus. 139

SECTION 5
Wettersteingebirge and Miemingergebirge 144
Stage 15   Solsteinhaus to Leutasch. 144
Stage 16   Leutasch to Ehrwald 148
Stage 17   Ehrwald to Schloss Fernstein castle 155

SECTION 6
Lechtal and Valluga 159
Stage 18   Schloss Fernstein castle to Anhalterhutte. 159
Stage 19   Anhalterhutte to Haselgehr. 164
Stage 20   Haselgehr to Steeg 170
Stage 21   Steeg to Stuttgarterhutte 175
Stage 22   Stuttgarterhutte to Ulmerhutte. 181
Stage 23   Ulmerhutte to St Anton am Arlberg. 183
Stage U22   Steeg to Leutkircherhutte. 187

SECTION 7
Lechtaler Alpen Hohenweg 190
Stage A17   Schloss Fernstein castle to Loreahutte 190
Stage A18   Loreahutte to Anhalterhutte. 192
Stage A19   Anhalterhutte to Hanauerhutte 194
Stage A20   Hanauerhutte to Wurttembergerhaus 197
Stage A21   Wurttembergerhaus to Memmingerhutte. 201
Stage A22   Memmingerhutte to Ansbacherhutte. 204
Stage A23   Ansbacherhutte to Kaiserjochhaus 206
Stage A24   Kaiserjochhaus to St Anton am Arlberg 208

APPENDIX A   Distances and timings. 212
APPENDIX B   Suggested 15-day and 21-day schedules 223
APPENDIX C   Tourist offices. 226
APPENDIX D   Useful contacts. 228
APPENDIX E   Glossary of German geographic terms 231

Map key

-----	border	▬▬▬	ridge
———	road	▲	peak
-•-•-•-	train/tram/funicular	✕	col
|- - - -🚠	cablecar	⬆	private refuges/hotels/ guest houses
|———🚡	chairlift	⬆	alpine club refuges
———	easy stages	🍴	meals/refreshments
- - - -	easy stages (alternative)	⛪	church
———	normal stages	✦	monument
- - - -	normal stages (alternative)	◠	cave or disused mine
———	challenging stages	·	reference point
- - - -	challenging stages (alternative)	●	station/bahnhof
———	stages by bus	❶	information
- - - - -	stages by train/tram/ funicular	Pinegg 675	altitude in metres
|- - - -🚠	stages by cablecar	←	direction arrow
|———🚡	stages by chairlift	†	hilltop cross
↑↑↑↑	{ direction of route		

Contour colour key

⬜	3000m+
⬜	2500–3000m
⬜	2000–2500m
⬜	1500–2000m
⬜	1000–1500m
⬜	500–1000m
⬜	0–500m

Other symbols:

Ⓢ start
Ⓕ finish
▨ urban area
▨ woods
▨ lake
〰 river

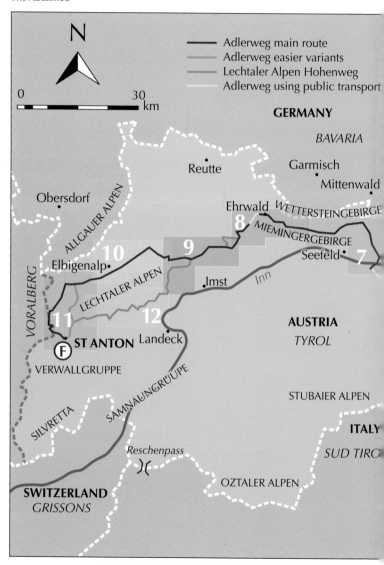

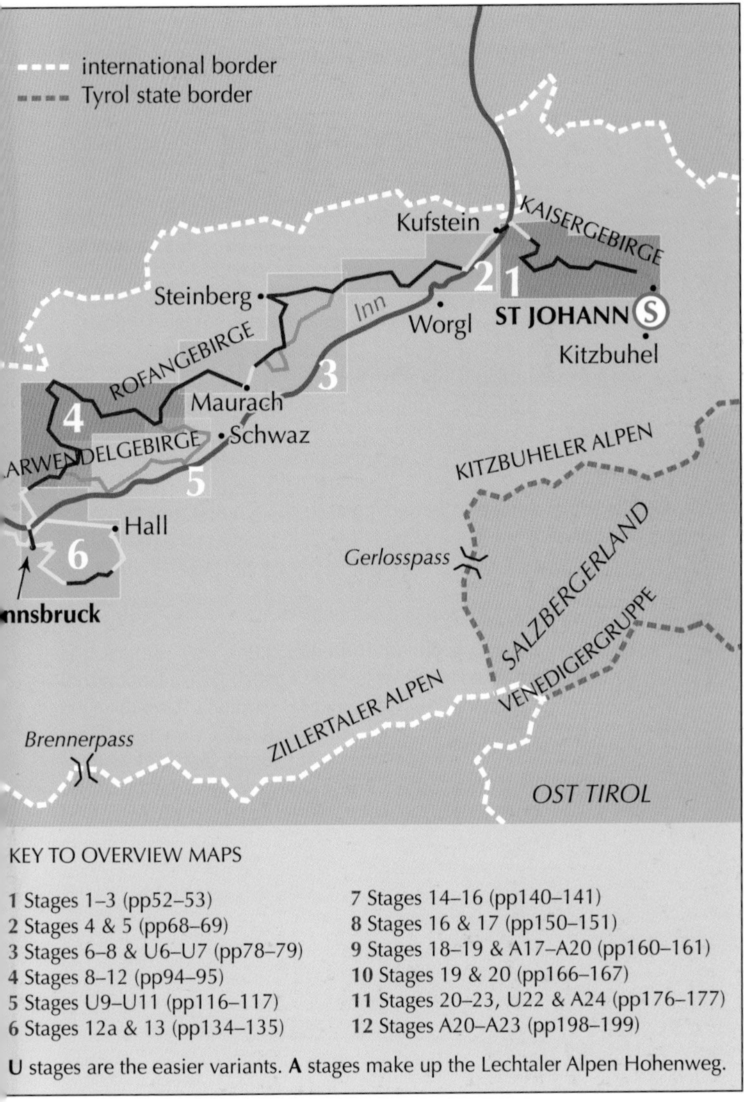

--- international border
-■-■- Tyrol state border

Kufstein

KAISERGEBIRGE

Steinberg

ROFANGEBIRGE

Inn

Worgl

ST JOHANN Ⓢ

Kitzbuhel

Maurach

•Schwaz

KARWENDELGEBIRGE

KITZBUHELER ALPEN

•Hall

Gerlosspass

SALZBERGERLAND

nnsbruck

VENEDIGERGRUPPE

Brennerpass

ZILLERTALER ALPEN

OST TIROL

KEY TO OVERVIEW MAPS

1 Stages 1–3 (pp52–53)
2 Stages 4 & 5 (pp68–69)
3 Stages 6–8 & U6–U7 (pp78–79)
4 Stages 8–12 (pp94–95)
5 Stages U9–U11 (pp116–117)
6 Stages 12a & 13 (pp134–135)

7 Stages 14–16 (pp140–141)
8 Stages 16 & 17 (pp150–151)
9 Stages 18–19 & A17–A20 (pp160–161)
10 Stages 19 & 20 (pp166–167)
11 Stages 20–23, U22 & A24 (pp176–177)
12 Stages A20–A23 (pp198–199)

U stages are the easier variants. **A** stages make up the Lechtaler Alpen Hohenweg.

Looking back to Birkkarspitze from Birkkarklamm gorge (Stage 11) (photo: Christine Gordon)

INTRODUCTION

There are two ways to soar among the magnificent peaks of the Tyrolean Alps. One is in an aeroplane as you fly into Innsbruck. The other, more challenging and exciting, is to follow the Adlerweg as it crosses the entire length of the Tyrol from St. Johann in Tirol in the east, to St. Anton am Arlberg in the west. Not only will you experience the Wilder Kaiser, Brandenberg, Rofan, Karwendel, and Lechtaler Alps close up, but you should also have spectacular distant views of Austria's other principal mountain ranges including Grossglockner, Grossvenediger, and the Tuxer and Stubai Alps. As a bonus, you will pass immediately below the towering south face of Zugspitze,

Bavaria's (and Germany's) highest mountain.

The main route of the Adlerweg is a 300km (188-mile) long-distance path traversing the Austrian Tyrol, keeping mostly to the mountains that form the northern side of Inntal, the Inn valley. It is made up of 23 principal stages, with a total height gain of nearly 17,000m. In addition, there are six easier variant stages that avoid the more airy parts, and eight more difficult 'Alpine' stages that provide an alternative high-level route through the Lechtaler Alps. Well maintained and waymarked throughout, the Adlerweg follows established mountain and valley tracks and allows you to reach the

Eagle motif found at key points along the Adlerweg

tops of two mountains, Rofanspitze (2259m) and Birkkarspitze (2749m). Accessible to walkers of all abilities, it can be completed by a fit walker in 15 days, although if you wish to take things more gently, and allow time to visit attractions en route, it would be best to allow three weeks. Most of the stages are well connected by public transport (train, postbus, cablecar and chairlift), making it possible to tackle shorter trips as day excursions or weekend overnight breaks.

The path was conceived and implemented by the Tyrol regional tourist organisation, who named it the Eagle's Way (*adler* being German for 'eagle') as, when overlaid on the map, its silhouette appears in the shape of an eagle, the outspread wings of which reach from one end of the Tyrol to the other, with Innsbruck, in the middle, as its head. The proud eagle is said to represent the feelings of freedom and independence, power and wisdom, grandeur and dignity, which you can experience by hiking the Eagle's Way. Since the introduction of the main route, the project has grown as offshoots from the path have spread right across the Tyrol: the eagle has grown legs. There is even a separate 'Eaglet' path of eight stages in Ost Tirol. The complete Adlerweg network now includes 126 stages with a vertical rise of about 87,000m. This guide concentrates on the 23-stage main route, plus the six 'easier' variant stages and eight 'harder' Alpine high-level stages.

Hiking in the Tyrol would not be complete without Austria's legendary hospitality and native cuisine. Since overnight accommodation in the form of serviced mountain *hutten*, inns, guesthouses or hotels can be found at the end of each day's walk, all you will need to carry is a sheet sleeping bag. Everywhere along the way there are convenient places to eat and drink. These range from simple alpine pasture huts in the mountains, offering locally produced fare, to award-winning restaurants in the towns and valleys. Indeed the accommodation and refreshment opportunities are so well spaced that, with a little forward planning, it is possible to walk the whole route without once needing to take a picnic lunch. On most stages, frequent water fountains and springs provide a safe source of drinking water.

A wide variety of animals and plants can be found. The lower meadows are carpeted with wild flowers in late spring, while once the snow disappears the upper slopes come alive with alpine plants, including edelweiss and gentian. Chamois, ibex and marmots can be seen throughout the route. However, as you are walking the Eagle's Way, the creature you will most want to find is likely to be the eponymous golden eagle. Keep a good lookout and you may see one soaring around the highest peaks. If, however, wild eagles prove illusive, the route passes Innsbruck's Alpine zoo, where there are two captive golden eagles.

Golden eagle in Innsbruck Alpen zoo (Stage 12a)

Croatia, Slovenia, Italy, Switzerland and Liechtenstein. Its position with the Danube, one of Europe's most important waterways, to the north, and the Brenner, the most accessible alpine pass, to the south, has made Austria the crossroads of central Europe.

During the 18th and 19th centuries, Austria's political, economic and military significance surpassed its modest size. After the turning back of Islamic incursions into Europe at the battle of Vienna (1683), a long period of rule by one family enabled Austria to maintain strong stable government and build a pan-European

Portrait of Hapsburg Empress Maria Theresa in Hofburg gallery, Innsbruck (Stage 12a)

The Tyrol tourist organisation describes the Adlerweg as 'arguably the most beautiful long-distance trail in Austria'. Does it live up to this claim? That is for you to decide. Walk it and see!

BACKGROUND

Austria

Located in the centre of the continent straddling the Alps, Austria is Europe's 17th largest country by size, and, with 8.3 million inhabitants, its 18th by population. It shares borders with Germany (with which it also shares a common language), the Czech Republic, Hungary, empire. The Hapsburg emperors ruled until defeat in World War 1 led to the break-up of the Austro-Hungarian Empire by the Treaty of Versailles in 1919.

A period of economic and political uncertainty during the 1920s and 1930s, (when many mountain refuges fell into disrepair), was followed by the Anschluss political union with Germany in 1938 and Austrian participation on the Axis side in World War 2. After the war, government was briefly divided between the victorious allied powers until the current republic was established in 1955. Austria joined the EU in 1995 and the

Interior of St Leonhard's Kapelle, Barnstatt (Stage 2)

subsequent signing of the Schengen Agreement led to the removal of border controls.

Austria is a federal republic of nine states. The majority of the population lives in four lowland states, including the capital Vienna, to the north and east of the country. Population density in the alpine states of the south and west, including Tyrol, is much lower.

Tyrol

Tyrol sits southwest of the bulk of Austria, between the states of Salzburg (east) and Voralberg (west). Its dominant feature is the deep west-to-east gash of the Inn valley between the north limestone Alps (Nordlichen Kalkalpen) and the central high Alps, with most of the 700,000 population living along this axis. Tyrol's northern border, with Germany, runs through the N Kalkalpen, and its southern, Italian, border through the central Alps.

> **Note** Throughout this guide the English spelling of Tyrol is used, except for proper nouns such as 'Count of Tirol', 'Sankt Johann in Tirol' or 'Tirol Werbung', where the German *Tirol* is used.

Tyrol's emergence as an identifiable state began in the 11th century when the Counts of Tirol from Meran (today Merano in northern

Italy) gradually extended their control over the whole region. When the last Count (or rather Countess) died heirless, control passed to the Austrian Hapsburgs with Tyrol becoming part of Austria in 1363. Apart from a brief period of Bavarian rule during the Napoleonic wars it has remained Austrian ever since. However, Tyrol today is much smaller than Hapsburg Tyrol, as the peace treaties that concluded WW1 transferred sovereignty over Sud Tirol and Triente to Italy.

Apart from Reutte in the northwest and Kitzbuhel in the east, the main towns spread along the Inn valley from Kufstein and Schwaz in the lower valley, through Innsbruck in the centre, to Imst and Landeck in the upper valley. By far the largest town is the state capital, Innsbruck.

Tyrol is a region of open countryside. Only 13% of the state has been developed for human habitation, with 35% forest, 30% pasture and 22% barren mountains. As a result the Tyrolean economy has been based on agriculture (mostly dairy farming), timber and mining (silver, lead, zinc, salt, limestone, silica sand and shale oil). Secondary industries have grown up using these raw materials, including wooden building materials, glass, cement and chemicals. Other light industry, originally based upon the ready availability of power from mountain streams but now using hydro-electric power, includes iron smelting, agricultural tools and machinery, railway carriages and electric power generators. In the 20th century, year round

Inn valley and North Kalkalpen ranges from Lechtaler Alpen to Karwendelgebirge, seen from Patscherkofel (Stage 13)

tourism (winter sports and summer touring) became a major part of the economy, while one of the largest employers in Innsbruck is the university.

THE ADLERWEG

The Adlerweg is a project promoted by Tirol Werbung (the state tourism promotional organisation) to encourage walkers to explore more of the region. It came to fruition in 2005 with the opening of the main route between Sankt Johann in Tirol, in the east of Tyrol, and Sankt Anton am Arlberg, on the western border with Voralberg. The route has no 'new' paths, being a series of existing paths and tracks linked by common signposting, usually by means of adding an Adlerweg motif to existing signposts.

The 23 stages of the main route have varying degrees of difficulty, although none requires climbing skills or equipment. Four of the stages are graded 'black' (difficult), although these have parallel easier alternatives. In addition, the Adlerweg makes use of the Lechtaler Alpen *Hohenweg* (high-level route) to provide a challenging alternative to the stages through the Lechtal valley.

There is, however, a political dimension to the project. Tirol Werbung is funded by regional government and by payments from all of the local government areas

(*gemeinde*) in the region. As a result, there was pressure to ensure the route visited as many gemeinde as possible. This has had two effects. Firstly, the route makes occasional deviations to visit villages off the direct route (Steinberg am Rofan in Stages 6/7 is the most obvious example). Secondly, the project was extended by the addition of 88 regional paths that form a series of legs running off the original route, thus taking the Adlerweg name into many other parts of Tyrol.

As a result, a degree of confusion has crept in. Mapmakers have been encouraged to add 'Adlerweg' or the eagle motif to their maps of the region. This has been done without discriminating between main route, easier variants, alpine high route and regional extensions, with 'Adlerweg' now popping up all over the map, making it difficult to identify the correct route. Furthermore, there are path junctions where both forks are signposted as Adlerweg!

One aspect of the Adlerweg that stands out, making it different from most other long-distance paths, is the use made of various modes of public transport to speed access to and descent from the mountains. As a result you will encounter three cablecars, three chairlifts, three trains, a funicular, a tram and a bus, all integrated into the path. It is possible to avoid some of the cablecars and chairlifts, and this guide indicates where such options occur.

Alpenpark sign in Karwendelgebirge (Stages 8–12)

NATIONAL PARKS AND PROTECTED AREAS

Although going through no designated national parks, much of the route is through areas with a high level of environmental protection or national forest. The Wilderkaiser, Karwendel, Arnspitze and most of Lechtal valley are *naturschutzgebieten* (NSG, nature protected areas) while other places are *landschaftsschutzgebieten* (LSG, similar to Areas of Special Scientific Interest in the UK). Brandenberg and Tegestal are national forests managed by Osterreichische Bundesforste (OBF). Proposals have been made to create national parks, but this high level of protection has been blocked by opposition from hunting interests, which are strong in Tyrol. Camping, lighting fires, disturbing wildlife or removing plants are prohibited in these areas.

PREPARATION

When to go

The Adlerweg is a summer walk with a season from mid-June to early October, although after heavy winter snowfall significant snow may remain at higher altitudes until mid-July, with early season falls commencing in early September. In a few locations, snow can remain all year. Opening and closing dates of mountain refuges and restaurants reflect the walkability of the paths, with refuges on the highest stages not opening until late June/early July and closing from mid-September. The most popular period for walking in Tyrol is mid-July to late August, and this is when you may encounter busy refuges, particularly those such as Karwendelhaus that coincide with the popular Vital Route mountain bike trail. You will meet very few walkers actually following the Adlerweg, although you will encounter many day walkers and even some walking the Munich to Venice long-distance route. Parts of the walk can be attempted in winter, but as this requires specialist skills and equipment it is not covered in this guide.

Apart from late lying snow, or early snowfalls, the going underfoot is usually excellent. The underlying stratum is limestone, resulting in good drainage with very few places prone to boggy conditions. After rain, or in mist, rocks can get very slippery and some of the stages over exposed rock can become treacherous. These parts of the trail are usually protected by fixed steel cables providing security in slippery conditions.

How long will it take?
The Adlerweg is not a walk to take lightly. It is possible to walk the entire route in 15 days, but this requires an average of seven hours' walking every day, covering above 20km, mostly above 1000m and sometimes above 2000m. To achieve this daily distance and ascent at altitude you need a good

---

HOLIDAYS IN AUSTRIA

There are a number of Austrian national holidays during the summer. On these days banks are closed and public transport operates *feiertage* (holiday) timetables, which are usually the same as Sunday schedules.

- Easter: variable, late March to late April
- May day: 1 May
- Ascension day: variable, May
- Whit Monday: variable, mid-May to mid-June
- Corpus Christi: variable, late May to late June
- Assumption day: 15 August
- National day: 26 October
- All Saints day: 1 November

School summer holidays run from mid-July to mid-September. Most towns and villages have summer festival days, and from mid-September to early October many villages celebrate Almabetriebsfest, when cows are welcomed back from summer mountain pastures (see box in Stage 21). In Innsbruck, the battle of Bergisel is commemorated on 14 August.

level of fitness. If you wish to take it more gently, five hours walking, covering 14km per day, will enable you to complete the walk in three weeks. Moreover, this will allow you time to see more of the region and visit a number of attractions passed en route such as a cruise on Achensee, a visit to the Alpen zoo or a cablecar to the summit of Zugspitze.

Each of the 23 stages can be walked in a day, most in less than this, allowing one and a half or two stages to be combined on most days. However a few stages, particularly Stage 11 (the crossing of Birkkarspitze from Karwendelhaus to Hallerangeralm),

The Adlerweg climbs into Rofangebirge through Schauertalkar to reach Schauertalsattel (Stage 7)

take a full day. Appendix B gives a suggested schedule showing which stages can be combined to walk the path in either 15 or 21 days.

With a few exceptions, which are shown in the text, it is not usually necessary to book ahead. Indeed Alpenverein (AV) refuges only require reservations from groups and recommend other members not to book, as places are guaranteed. However if you want a bedroom rather than a dormitory place, booking could be useful. For locations such as Hintersteinersee, Kaiserhaus, Fernstein and Bschlabs, where there is no AV accommodation and only one private guesthouse/inn/hotel, reservations are recommended. The same applies to private refuges with only a small number of beds, particularly at weekends.

Tourist offices

Tourist offices operate at both regional and local levels. Tirol Werbung in Innsbruck is responsible for marketing Tyrol as a tourist destination and part of this role involves setting up, managing and promoting the Adlerweg network of paths. They produce a map and guide to all 128 stages and through their website www.adlerweg. tirol.at individual Kompass 1:50,000 maps of each stage can be downloaded. While the guidebook provides excellent outline information, it is not sufficiently detailed to walk the path as only one paragraph is allocated to each stage.

A popular pastime of Tyrolean walkers is to collect the passport type stamps available at every refuge and most hotels and guesthouses. To encourage Adlerweg walkers to participate, Tirol Werbung has produced a *stempelbuch* (stamping book) that can be obtained from their offices in Innsbruck. When you have completed your walk, you can claim an eagle pin, in gold, silver or bronze colours depending on how many stamps you have collected. Alternatively, a few pages at the end of this book have been left clear for you to collect your stamps.

Every town and most villages have their own local tourist office, which can provide local maps and full details of accommodation and events in their area. Opening times vary and smaller offices may not be open at weekends. Staff are generally very helpful and speak good English. Advice is provided on all grades of accommodation and most offices will call to check vacancies and make reservations. They cannot make reservations 'out of area' but are usually willing to phone the relevant local office and relay your requirements. Contact details for all tourist offices can be found in Appendix C.

Alpine Club

Founded in 1862, the Oesterreichischer Alpenverein (OeAV, Austrian Alpine Club) now has nearly 400,000 members involved in all kinds of mountain sports. Among other activities, it is responsible for building, maintaining and modernising a large number of mountain refuges, waymarking and maintaining footpaths, producing maps and guidebooks and aiding the independent rescue service. It works closely with the Deutsche Alpenverein (DAV, German Alpine Club) which owns and operates the majority of mountain refuges on the Adlerweg. Many of these were built by DAV sections early in the 20th century to provide mountain recreational facilities for members throughout Germany. After WW2 they were placed under Austrian control, but since the sixties have been returned to their former owners.

Facilities can be used by anyone, but members obtain specific benefits including substantial discounts on accommodation and guaranteed overnight space in club refuges, annual rescue and repatriation insurance and

A typical Alpenverein refuge – Lamsenjochhutte (Stage 8)

maps and guidebooks at discounted prices. Benefits are available on a reciprocal basis with other national alpine clubs, including DAV.

If you are planning to walk the Adlerweg, and are not a member of an alpine club, you are strongly recommended to join OeAV. The easiest way to do this is to become a member of AAC (UK), also known as Sektion Britannia. Contact details are in Appendix D. AAC (UK) is a fully-fledged section of OeAV with over 6000 members. Annual membership in 2011 cost £42, with a 25% reduction for seniors (over 60) and juniors (under 16).

GETTING THERE

By air is the only way of getting from the UK to the start of the Adlerweg in one day. There are direct flights by various airlines from a number of UK airports to Munich, Innsbruck or Salzburg.

- *From Munich airport*, frequent S-bahn trains (S8 to Munich Ost (37min) and S1 to Munich Hbf (40min)), link the airport with the DB German rail network. Regular DB trains connect Munich with Rosenheim, Kufstein and Worgl in the Inn valley. OBB (Austrian) trains connect Worgl with St Johann.
- *From Salzburg airport*, bus route 2 runs to Salzburg Hbf from where OBB trains enable you to reach St Johann via Bischofshofen.
- *From Innsbruck airport* there is a bus to Innsbruck Hbf for regular OBB trains to Worgl and St Johann.

Return from St Anton by OBB trains to Innsbruck then connect for Munich via Kufstein or Garmish, or for Salzburg via Kufstein or via Bischofshofen. An alternative return route from St Anton is via OBB and SBB (Swiss) direct trains to Zurich. Frequent trains connect Zurich Hbf with Zurich airport, where various airlines fly to UK airports.

Travel by rail will take two days, with an overnight break necessary in Cologne, Frankfurt or Munich. The best route is to take the Eurostar from London to either Brussels or Paris.

- *From London St Pancras to Brussels* by Eurostar (approx 2-hourly), then Brussels to Cologne or Frankfurt by Thalys or DB ICE (approx 2-hourly) and Cologne or Frankfurt to Munich by DB (hourly, more than one route). Then travel Munich to Worgl by DB, with OBB connection at Worgl for St Anton.

- *From London St Pancras to Paris Nord* by Eurostar (approx hourly) and short walk to Paris Est for trains to Stuttgart by SNCF (TGV) or DB (ICE). Then Stuttgart to Munich by DB (approx hourly) and continue as above.

Return from St Anton by OBB trains via Innsbruck to Munich; or via Bregenz, Lindau, Ulm and connect for Frankfurt; then retrace your outward journey.

Tickets are available from DB or Rail Europe. Contact details are in Appendix D.

You can catch a tram from Bergisel to reach the start of Stage 13 in Igls (photo: Christine Gordon)

By road using Eurotunnel/car ferry via Calais. Autoroute/autobahn across Belgium and Germany to Munich and Kufstein, then local roads to St Johann via Elmau. Total distance Calais–St Johann 1100km. Driving time is at least 11hrs. Leaving your car in St Johann you can return by train from St Anton via Innsbruck and Worgl to pick it up.

Intermediate access

- Hintersteinersee is reached by bus, four times a day from Scheffau, which is served by buses between St Anton and Worgl.
- Kufstein: station on main line between Munich and Innsbruck. Bus services to St Johann and Innsbruck.
- Kaiserhaus: bus from Kramsach/Rattenberg, which is served by local trains between Kufstein and Innsbruck.
- Steinberg: bus from Achenkirk, which is served by bus from Jenbach changing at Maurach; or from Munich by BOB train to Tegernsee and bus to Achenkirk.
- Achensee (Maurach/Pertisau): bus (hourly) or Achenseebahn train (four/five per day) from Jenbach main line. Also by train and bus from Munich via Achenkirk.
- Absam: frequent local buses from Hall and Innsbruck.
- Innsbruck: airport with direct flights from the UK. Main line station with international trains to Munich, Vienna, Salzburg,

In high season a vintage bus runs between Pertisau and Gramaialm (Stage 8)

23

Verona, Milan and Zurich. Many bus services.

- Hochzirl/Seefeld/Geissenbach/ Scharnitz: stations served by trains on Mittenwald line between Innsbruck and Garmish/ Munich.
- Leutasch: bus from Seefeld.
- Ehrwald/Lermoos: trains from Innsbruck or Munich changing at Garmish.
- Fernstein: bus service between Imst/Nassereith and Lermoos/ Reutte.
- Bschlabs/Boden: three buses per day from Elmen in Lechtal valley.
- Lechtal valley: regular bus service between Reutte and Steeg calling at villages along the Lechtal valley. Reutte is served by trains from Innsbruck or Munich, changing at Garmish.
- Kaisers: six buses per day from Steeg.
- Steeg: buses from St Anton, changing at Lech.

NAVIGATION

Path grading

Throughout the Tyrol a standard system is used to grade the level of experience, skills, fitness and equipment required to walk mountain paths. There are three grades: *wanderweg*, *roter bergweg* and *schwarzer bergweg*. The system is colour coded, with white (wanderweg), red (roter bergweg) or black (schwarzer bergweg), usually appearing in a small circle on signposts. The official grading appears in this guide in the introduction to each stage. The grade relates to the most difficult part you will encounter in a stage. There is one exception, in Stage 4, where despite the stage being classified red, the ridge walk section from Koglhorndl to Hundsalmjoch is graded black. An alternative route is signposted avoiding this section.

- Wanderweg (white) are easily accessible footpaths, generally wide with only slight gradients. There is no exposure, and neither a head for heights nor mountain equipment is needed. Four stages are classified wanderweg.
- Roter bergweg (red) are trails with a moderate level of difficulty, sometimes steep or narrow with short cable-aided sections possible. Surefootedness, a reasonable head for heights and appropriate physical condition are required. No specialist mountain equipment is needed, although a good pair of walking boots and appropriate clothing is essential. The majority of Adlerweg stages are roter bergweg.
- Schwarzer bergweg (black) are steeper, more difficult stages, often narrow with aided scrambling sections and exposure to steep drops. Experience of mountain walking is essential, together with a reasonable level of physical fitness, surefootedness

and a good head for heights. However, these stages are walks or scrambles, not climbs, so no specialist mountaineering equipment is needed. There are four schwarzer bergweg stages on the main Adlerweg, although these can be avoided with easier alternatives, plus four more on the Lechtaler Alpen Hohenweg.

Waymarking

The Adlerweg network is marked with a standard series of signs and signposts. At the beginning of most stages is a signboard showing the whole stage together with timing, distance and height difference. En route signposting using yellow fingerposts is almost universal and excellent. These fingerposts can be found at most path junctions, and even in remote locations they leave little doubt as to which path to take. They usually show the next few destinations together with estimated walking times and path grade (white/red/black). The Adlerweg is identified on these signs by an eagle silhouette motif, and often by name. Occasionally, older style black and white signboards are encountered, although these are steadily being replaced.

Between fingerposts, the path is identified by the use of red and white paint flashes on convenient surfaces such as rocks, trees, walls and buildings. These provide waymarking over difficult ground and are essential through forests, across scree and in open pasture where the path may sometimes be indistinct. Occasionally small cairns mark the route, but in misty conditions, paint

Yellow fingerposts showing the Adlerweg are found at almost every path junction

25

flashes are considerably more visible. On some stages, where the Adlerweg uses another established path such as Wilder Kaiser Steig in Stage 2, other coloured paint flashes may be encountered. In Voralberg, Stage 22, yellow/white flashes are used for wanderweg, red/white for roter bergweg, and blue/white for schwarzer bergweg.

GPS

All maps listed are GPS compatible under WGS 84 with co-ordinates in both degrees/minutes and UTM. The OeAV CD/ROM maps can be downloaded to GPS. Most refuges publish their GPS co-ordinates on their websites and a complete list is published in OeAV hutten guide. An increasing number of signposts show GPS co-ordinates.

Guidebooks

Tirol tourist board in Innsbruck has produced a 96-page summary guide and accompanying map to all 128 main, alternative and regional stages. While this gives an overview of each stage, it is not suitable to take with you when walking. The first edition (2007) was published in English and German versions, but the second edition (2010) is available in German only. It is available from Tirol Werbung, Maria Theresien Strasse 55, Innsbruck 6010 (www.adlerweg.tirol.at).

Bruckmann have published a 144-page guide to all main, variant and regional paths, with a detailed description of the main stages with full colour mapping, plus variant

Signs at the start and finish of each stage

and regional paths in summary form. It is available in German only: *Der Adlerweg*, Stefanie Holzer (2009) ISBN 978-3-7654-4796-9 Bruckmann Verlag, Postfach 40 02 09, D-80702 Munchen (www.bruckmann.de).

Alpenverein Hutte Book contains details of all alpine refuges in Austria, Germany and Sud Tirol. It is in German with an English key explaining symbols and is available from Austrian Alpine Club UK, 12a North St, Wareham, Dorset BH20 4AG (www.aacuk.org.uk).

MAPS

This guide is not intended for use on its own. It is essential to have walking maps at a scale of 1:50,000 or 1:25,000. Maps from three publishers cover the route, and sheet numbers

are shown for each stage. However, there are differences between the published maps in terms of scale, coverage and accuracy, as well as when information was researched.

Oesterreichischer Alpenverein (AV) maps cover almost 90% of the route at 1:25,000. There is no coverage of the walk-in from St Johann, and the Brandenberger Stages 4, 5 and part of Stages 6 and U6, with Stage 13 covered only at 1:50,000. These maps give the most comprehensive coverage of the Adlerweg, but 14 sheets are required (13 AV plus one from another publisher for the Brandenberger Alpen). They have been revised from original OeAV maps to update land use, path networks and settlements, and do show the Adlerweg. Contours are at 20m intervals overlaid with black hairline

The Adlerweg crosses Gruba bowl from Rofanspitze, just visible right of centre, passing beneath Rosskopf (Stage 7)

depiction of rock features. The maps are GPS compatible with UTM grid. Sheets required are: 8, 6, 5/3, 5/2, 5/1, 4/3, 4/2, 4/1, 3/4, 3/3, 3/2 and 2/2 (all 1:25,000) and 31/5 (1:50,000) plus Kompass 28.

A DVD is available of all OeAV maps. From this you can print your own strip maps of the route, at an enhanced scale (1:10,000), with considerable weight and space saving compared with carrying printed maps.

Freytag and Berndt (FB) cover the route in six sheets at 1:50,000. In addition, there is a 1:25,000 map of Karwendel that can be used instead of the 1:50,000. Maps come with an enclosed booklet (in German) of tourist information, path and walking routes, mountain refuges and guesthouses, and GPS details of key points shown on the maps. All sheets are updated regularly, using satellite photography plus information from tourist offices and alpine clubs, and are reissued at three-year intervals. Contours are at 100m intervals. Maps are GPS compatible with UTM grid. Sheets required are: 301, 321, 322, 241, 352 and 351. Sheet 5322 (1:25,000) can be used instead of 322.

Kompass (K) cover the route, either with two maps at 1:25,000, two maps at 1:35,000 and three maps at 1:50,000; or with six maps all at 1:50,000. The maps come with a booklet giving details of towns, villages, mountain paths and accommodation. Contours are at 40m intervals, and the maps are GPS compatible

with UTM grid. Details and path markings are clearer than on Freytag and Berndt maps. The larger scale maps are simply enlargements of the 1:50,000, making them easier to read but with no greater detail. The Adlerweg is shown on all sheets. Sheets required are: 9, 28, 26, 36, 5 and 24 (all 1:50,000); or 09 and 026 (1:25,000), 027 and 036 (1:35,000) and 28, 5 and 24 (1:50,000).

> **Recommended maps to cover the entire Adlerweg route**
>
> **1:25,000**
> * AV 8, 6, 5/3, 5/2, 5/1, 4/3, 4/2, 4/1, 3/4, 3/3, 3/2 and 2/2
>
> **1:50,000**
> * AV 31/5, Kompass 28

Tourist office maps: in addition to the published maps, Kompass have produced maps for some of the local tourist organisations, with a 1:50,000 map on one side and a local map or panorama on the reverse. These are available free from local tourist offices. Kompass maps are also used by Tirol Werbung for their strip maps of each stage, and these can be downloaded free from www.adlerweg.tirol. at. Local tourist offices also produce street maps of the towns and villages passed through.

All the maps are available from leading map shops, including Stanfords in London and The Map Shop in Upton upon Severn, and are widely available in Austria. OeAV maps and the DVD can also be obtained from either OeAV in Innsbruck or OeAV Britannia Section at www.aacuk.org.uk at a discounted price for AV members.

ACCOMMODATION

Places to stay overnight on the Adlerweg vary from basic mountain refuges to five star hotels. In general you will need to stay in refuges when in the mountains, while on evenings when the path leads down into the valleys, you will find a variety of bed & breakfasts, guesthouses, inns and hotels. Such a network of accommodation means that the need to camp is rare and there are very few official camping sites. However, a tent is not needed as you are never more than a day's walk from accommodation, and usually only half a day.

Mountain refuges

Austrian mountains are well provided with a huge network of serviced mountain walkers' refuges, called in German *hutte* (pl *hutten*). Refuges are either operated by the Austrian (OeAV) or German (DAV) Alpenverein (alpine clubs), or are privately run. On or near to the Adlerweg and its variants there are 23 Alpenverein refuges and 14 private ones.

Alpine club refuges are owned and managed by individual sections of Alpenverein and this is often reflected in their names, such as Bayreutherhutte and Stuttgarterhutte. The UK section has no refuges of its own, but members are encouraged to contribute to a fund that helps maintain some of the less well funded refuges. On the Adlerweg, Steinseehutte in the Lechtaler Alpen has been a beneficiary of this fund, contributing to the installation of solar heating and warm showers.

Refuges are graded according to their facilities, and this is reflected in the overnight price. Accommodation can be in individual rooms sleeping from two to eight, or in the slightly cheaper *lager*, a mixed-sex dormitory often in the roof space. Most refuges have hot water and many have hot showers for which there is a small charge. Blankets and pillows are provided, but guests are expected to provide their own sheets. Advance booking can be made, and this is required for large groups. At weekends in high season, some refuges, particularly those in the Karwendel, can be very full. However, AV members are guaranteed somewhere to sleep and a proportion of places are kept back for this purpose. At very busy times, spare mattresses and put-me-up beds can fill the dining rooms and corridors. Discounts of 30% to 50% on accommodation (not food) are made for AV members and for members of other national alpine clubs. Self-catering is not usually possible, except for Loreahutte (Stage A17), which is unserviced. Overall, AV refuges offer a warm, welcoming and good value place to eat and sleep.

Most private refuges offer similar facilities and services to AV refuges. Rooms may be a little less spartan, prices slightly higher with no discounts available to AV members and there are no guaranteed places. In some locations (at the top of Rofan cablecar or at Hallerangeralm, for instance) private and AV refuges stand in close proximity to each other, giving walkers a choice. It is recommended that AV members use the AV refuge while non-members should take the private option.

Wilde Bande Steig contours high above Isstal towards Stempeljoch col with Pfeiserspitze on the left (Stage 12)

Hotels, inns, guesthouses, bed & breakfast and youth hostels
Off the mountains, in the towns and villages and in the valleys, you will need to stay in commercial accommodation. Virtually all accommodation is vetted and graded by local tourist organisations and booking can be made through local tourist offices. Only two 'valley end' stages have only one accommodation option, Stage 5 at the Kaiserhaus inn and Stage 17 at the Fernstein Castle Hotel.

Hotels tend to be full service establishments with all facilities (restaurant, bar, sauna, gym and perhaps a pool). Inns, often called *haus* (although this term can also refer to some mountain refuges) are simpler, often in remote

locations, and usually have a restaurant. Guesthouses (*gasthof*) sometimes have a restaurant, but not always. B&Bs are private houses that take overnight guests. They have no restaurant, but do provide breakfast. They can usually be identified by a sign showing *zimmer frei* (room available). Inns, guesthouses and B&Bs can all offer very good value, sometimes no more expensive than mountain refuges. Prices usually include breakfast. There are only two youth hostels (*Jugendherberge*) on the Adlerweg, in Maurach and Innsbruck.

Camping

Much of the route is through protected areas where wild camping is prohibited. Wild camping is possible in a few places, but in general the availability of affordable mountain accommodation means very few Adlerweg walkers choose to camp. There are only six official campsites en route plus six others a short distance away.

Campsites en route are at Langkampfen, Maurach, Lermoos, Fernstein, Haselgehr and Elbigenalp. Campsites off-route can be found at St Johann, Kufstein, Innsbruck, Scharnitz, Leutasch and Ehrwald.

FOOD AND DRINK

Places to eat

The Adlerweg is well provided with places where walkers can find food and beverages. With one exception, all the refuges on the trail provide

Evening in a busy refuge – Karwendelhaus (Stages 10 and 11)

lunch and those with accommodation serve breakfast and dinner. (The exception is Loreahutte at the end of Stage A17, which is self-catering). In addition, there are a number of *almhutten* (pasture huts) providing lunchtime fare. Every town and village passed through has somewhere to eat, even tiny hamlets like Engalm (Stage 9) and Bschlabs (Stage 19) have *gaststatte*.

Refuges generally offer a choice of hot and cold meals for lunch and dinner, the variety, range and prices depending upon the size, popularity and accessibility of the refuge. Most have vehicular or goods lift access, although some (most notably Anhalterhutte at end of Stage 18) need supplies to be carried at least part way. Food is normally of the hearty/filling variety rather than gourmet cuisine. An inclusive three course set dinner with accommodation and breakfast is available (often only to prebooked AV members) in some refuges. Many establishments offer their own specialities, but as these depend upon particular wardens, who may change from year to year, they are not listed in this guide. Up to date information can usually be obtained from each refuge's web site or from the OeAV hutten guide. In the past specialities have included such things as free-range turkey (Hohlensteinhaus), game, Italian food, homemade cakes and even Nepalese cooking (Anhalterhutte).

Pasture huts (almhutten) provide a more limited lunchtime fare. Usually operated by the local farmer as a side venture, they typically serve *jausen* (cold meats, ham, cheese with bread and pickles) accompanied by fresh milk, fresh apple juice and other beverages. Produce is often home grown or reared. Opening hours are more limited than in refuges, with some opening weekends only, except in high season.

A restaurant usually indicates a slightly more formal environment with uniformed servers and starched table linen, whereas a gaststatte is generally a more relaxed local eatery. A *speisesaal* is a dining room usually within a hotel or guesthouse, while a *stube* is a dining room decorated in traditional style. An *imbisstube* is a snackbar.

With the exception of a few upmarket establishments in Innsbruck, meal prices in local restaurants are comparable with prices in refuges (they do not have the added costs of transportation and live-in labour). A wide range of Tyrolean, Austrian and international food is available. Many restaurants, but not all, have menus available in English. When you want to settle up, you can ask either 'zahlen bitte' ('can I pay please?') or for *die rechnung* (the bill). Tipping is not expected in Austrian restaurants, but it is customary to leave your small change.

Austrian/German food

Although the Adlerweg is entirely in Austria, many refuges are operated by German AV sections and some can only be supplied from the north (Bavarian) side of the mountains. The food and beverages you will encounter will thus be a mix of Tyrolean and Bavarian cuisine.

Refuges usually offer two choices of breakfast (*fruhstuck*): simple continental (bread, butter, jam and tea/coffee) or a larger version that includes these dishes plus cold meats and cheese. Boiled eggs may be available and sometimes fruit juice and breakfast cereals. In refuges, breakfast usually starts from 0700.

Lunch (*mittagessen*) from 1200 is the main meal of an Austrian day, although walkers often choose a lighter lunch, with the main meal in the evening. A typical Austrian snack, which may be taken from mid-morning until mid-afternoon, is a *jause*, a thick slice of bread topped with cheese (*kase*) or ham (*schinken*). A more substantial version consisting of a selection of meats or cheeses and bread (rather like a Ploughman's lunch) is served on a wooden platter and known as a *brettjause*. Plates of sausages and mustard (*wurst mit senf*) served with bread (*brot*) or bowls of goulash soup (beef stew flavoured with paprika) are widely available lunch snacks. Other soups include clear broths with strips of pancake, and cream soups such as *knoblauch* (garlic) or *zweibel* (onion).

Cakes (*kuchen*), which are often homemade (*hausgemacht*), accompany coffee during the afternoon. Typical Austrian cakes include *Sachertorte*, a chocolate and apricot

Jause *lunchtime snack with* hefeweizen *wheat beer*

creation that originated in the Hotel Sacher in Vienna, but can now be found almost anywhere. If you want to try the original recipe, Café Sacher has a branch in the entrance to the Hofburg in Innsbruck, which you pass on Stage 12a.

For the evening meal (*abendessen*), the mainstays of Tyrolean cooking are hearty simple dishes of meat and various kinds of savoury *knodel* (dense, tennis ball size dumplings), *kartoffel* (potatoes) or *spatzle* (noodles). The most common meat is from the pig (pork, gammon, bacon, ham), but you will also find beef or veal, chicken, turkey and occasionally lamb. Austria's most renowned dish, *Wiener schnitzel* (veal escalope fried in egg and breadcrumbs) is almost ubiquitous. Another Austrian speciality is *tafelspitz* (braised beef). Particularly Tyrolean is *grostl*, a hash made from leftover cooked pork, diced potatoes and onions fried in butter and topped with a fried egg. Hunting, which is widely practised in local forests, provides game such as venison (*reh*), chamois (*gams*) and boar (*wildschwein*), while anglers catch trout (*forelle*) from the rivers and pikeperch (*zander*) from the lakes. The most common vegetable is *sauerkraut* (pickled cabbage). Abendessen starts at 1800 in some refuges, but more typically from 1900.

The most common dessert is *strudel*, usually apple but sometimes apricot (*marillen*), poppy seed (*mohn*) or curd cheese (*topfen*). Two typically Tyrolean, and very substantial desserts, are *Germknodel*, a sweet dumpling filled with poppy seeds and plum jam, served with custard (vanilla sauce); and *Kaiserschmarrn*, a pancake made with raisins, which is served chopped and dusted with sugar.

Vegetarianism is still considered by many Austrians to be an exotic fad, and catering for vegetarians is rather hit or miss. In refuges, vegetarian fare is unlikely to be more than pasta with tomato sauce, *knodel* in cheese sauce or a veggie casserole.

Drinks

Tap water is usually safe to drink, and on the few occasions when it is not, you will always be told '*nicht trinkwasser*'. Water in refuges often comes straight from mountain springs. Many drinking fountains and water troughs, often drawing water from springs, can be found along the path, particularly at lower and middle levels. However as the underlying rock is mostly porous limestone, natural water sources at higher altitudes are often scarce and you should take water with you.

All the usual soft drinks (colas, lemonade, juices) are widely available. Austrian specialities include *Almdudler*, a drink made from mountain herbs and tasting of elderflower, often used as a mixer with white wine. A very refreshing soft drink is a mix of apple juice and sparkling water (*apfelgespritz* or *apfelschorle*). The

Grostl *(Tyrollean pork and potato hash)*

popular energy drink Red Bull origi-nated in Japan, but was introduced into Europe by an Austrian entrepre-neur who still has his head office near Salzburg. Pasture huts often sell milk straight from the dairy, although the milk in refuges is usually UHT.

Tyrol, like nearby Bavaria, is a beer consuming region and beer is available from a wide variety of local and national breweries. Many refuges, except those in the most remote loca-tions, have both bottled and draught beer. The main types of beer are German style lagers and *hefeweizen* (wheat beer). Wheat beer popularity is increasing and can be found in both *helles* (pale) and *dunkles* (dark) varie-ties. Very refreshing and slightly sweet tasting, wheat beer is unfiltered and thus naturally cloudy in appearance.

Beer is sold in a number of standard measures; *Pfiff* (200mm), *Kleines* or *Seidel* (300mm) and *Grosses* or *Halbe* (half litre). Hefeweizen is tradition-ally served in half litre, vase shaped glasses.

Radler (shandy, a blend of beer and lemonade) is a popular and refreshing drink that is always avail-able and, having only 50% of the alcohol content of beer is probably a better choice at lunchtime. *Apfelwein* (cider) made from apples can also be found.

Austria is a major wine produc-ing country, although almost all Austrian wine comes from the eastern part of the country, with little or no production in Tyrol. Most wine pro-duced is white with Gruner Veltliner the most commonly used grape

TYROLEAN FRUIT SCHNAPPS

There is a particularly wide selection of schnapps at Tuxerbauern distillery in Tulfes, near the bottom of the Glungezerbahn cablecar (Stage 13). An excellent souvenir, but not very practical to carry around. However as Tulfes is only a short bus trip from Innsbruck, you could always return at the end of your walk and pick up a bottle or two before travelling home.

along with Riesling, Muller Thurgau, Weissburgunder and Rulander. Red wine, mostly produced from Pinot Noir (Blauburgunder) or Zweigelt (Rotburger) grapes, is growing in popularity. Imported, mostly Italian, wines are readily available and often cheaper than Austrian wine. This is not surprising as Italian wine producing regions are closer to Tyrol than Austrian vineyards. Wine can be bought by the bottle, or as house wine (*offene weine*) by the glass or carafe in sizes *achtel* (125ml), *viertel* (250ml), *halbe* (half litre) and litre.

At the close of a meal, Austrians typically drink schnapps, a distillation of alcohol from a wide variety of fruits, berries and herbs. Tyrol is a major producer of fruit schnapps (typically about 40% alcohol) and fruit liqueurs (less strong, at about 20%). Small local suppliers often produce these (there are 20,000 registered schnapps distilleries in Austria) from fruits such as pear (*williams*), apricot (*marillen*), plum (*zwetschken*), and bilberry (*myrtille*). Particularly distinctive tastes are those of *krauter*, a distillation flavoured with herbs, and *enzian* from the root of the gentian flower. Schnapps is usually bottled commercially, although sometimes you will find local distillations decanted into unmarked bottles. Many refuges have a *haus schnapps*, sometimes home produced. Beware, quality and strength can vary greatly from sophisticated smoothness to throat burning firewater!

Coffee is the Austrian hot drink of choice. Legend has it that coffee was introduced in 1683 when retreating Ottoman troops left bags of beans behind after the Battle of Vienna. Coffee is served in a wide variety of styles. *Mokka* or *kleiner schwarzer* (small black) is similar to expresso, *kleiner brauner* (small brown) is served with milk; *verlangerter* (lengthened) is diluted with hot water; *melange* (mixed) is topped up with hot milk; while einspanner is topped with whipped cream. Italian styles such as cappuccino and café latte are also commonly served.

Tea is growing in popularity. *Schwarzer tee* (black tea or English breakfast tea) is widely available, along with a range of fruit and herbal teas. Tea is served with lemon. If you want it with cold milk, you need to ask for *tee mit kalt milch*. To warm yourself up on a cold day you could try hot chocolate with rum, a popular winter après-ski drink.

AMENITIES AND SERVICES

Shops

All towns and larger villages passed through have grocery stores, often small supermarkets, and many have pharmacies. Opening hours vary, but most open early. Grocery stores close at 1300 on Saturdays and stay closed all day Sunday. Clothing and outdoor equipment stores can be found in St Johann, Kufstein, Pertisau, Innsbruck, Leutasch, Ehrwald, Lermoos, Elbigenalp and St Anton.

Post offices

All towns and some villages have post offices. Opening hours vary.

Currency and banks

Austria changed from using Schillings to Euros in 2002. There are banks in St Johann, Kufstein, Unterlangkampfen, Maurach, Pertisau, Absam, Innsbruck, Igls, Weidach, Ehrwald, Lermoos, Elbigenalp, Haselgehr, Holzgau, Steeg and St Anton. Normal opening hours are 0800–1230 and 1330–1500 (weekdays only), with extended opening until 1730 on Thursdays. Most branches have ATM machines, which enable you to make transactions in English. Contact your bank before you leave home to activate your card for use in Austria.

Telephones

Austria has extensive mobile phone (*handi*) coverage, even in mountain areas where signals can often be received from the valleys below. Contact your network provider before you leave home to ensure your phone is enabled for foreign use and that you have the optimum price package. If you plan to make many local calls once you have arrived, it usually pays to obtain a local SIM card. The international dialling code for Austria is 0043. Some DAV refuges are contacted via Germany (international dialling code 0049).

An increasing number of hotels, guesthouses and even a few refuges make internet access available to guests, often free but sometimes for a small fee.

Electricity

Voltage is 220v, 50HzAC. Plugs are standard European two-pin round.

Bschlabs church from the opposite side of Bschlabertal (Stage 19)

THE NATURAL ENVIRONMENT

Physical geography

The Alps, which form a high mountain barrier between northern and southern Europe, are some of the youngest European mountains. They were formed approximately 50 million years ago, being pushed up by the collision of the African and European tectonic plates. The Alps run west to east through Austria and consist of three parallel mountain ranges, the high, mainly granite, central Alps flanked by the slightly lower northern and southern calcareous limestone chains. The Adlerweg traverses the most northerly of these, the Nordlichen Kalkalpen, following the range from east to west. For much of its length there are extensive views south across the deep glacial defile of the Inn valley with the higher permanently snow-capped central Alps on the horizon, and occasional views north across the Alpine foothills to the basin of the Danube beyond.

The chain is broken into a series of blocks by a number of north to south glacial river valleys that have broken through the mountains. As their name implies, the calcareous Alps are composed mostly of porous limestone, with the exact composition of this limestone varying from block to block. The two most significant geological aspects of the region are glaciation and karst country.

During the great ice ages, ice sheets covered all of central and northern Europe. As the ice retreated, great glaciers carved deep valleys through the Austrian Alps, the deepest and longest forming the Inn valley. Running east from the Engadine region of Switzerland right across Tyrol, where it separates the northern and central Alpine ranges, it reaches the Danube basin beyond Kufstein. Along its length, the Inn is joined by lateral glacial valleys flowing in from north and south. Most of the glaciers have long since melted and only a few remain, mostly in the high central Alps. The only remaining glacier encountered by the Adlerweg is Pazielferner above St Anton and upper Lechtal.

The enduring legacies left behind by the retreating glaciers are characteristic deep U-shaped valleys and morainic lakes. Throughout the walk you will be able to trace old glacial flows, from smooth bowl-shaped cirques surrounded on three sides by high jagged mountains, down stepped valleys blocked by terminal moraines containing either morainic lakes or the dried up beds of earlier lakes. The descent from Birkkarspitze (Stage 11) is almost a geography lesson with every kind of glacial feature on show.

The receding glaciers stripped much of the topsoil, leaving large areas of smooth limestone exposed. The steady slow erosion of this bare limestone by acidic rainwater causes limestone pavements to be formed. While karst pavements are seen on the surface (notably above Zireineralm, Stage U6), most karst

Glacial cirque below Birkkarspitze (Stage 11)

features are hidden below ground in a series of sinkholes and cave systems. Zireinersee lake (Stages 7 and U6) is a karst lake with no visible outlet, while the Hundsalm Eishohle cave (Stage 4) is part of a karst cave system.

Walking the Adlerweg, you will encounter a few morainic lakes, some trapped by terminal moraines and some by lateral. The most notable is Achensee, the unique geography of which is described in Stage 8, while the descent from Fern pass (Stage 17) provides excellent views of a series of turquoise coloured lakes, each trapped by its own moraine. Lateral lakes line the Inn valley between Kramsach and Worgl. Dried up lake-beds far exceed actual lakes, the most obvious being the Moos (between Ehrwald and Lermoos, Stage 17) and the Hinterautal valley (Stage 11). Extensive beaches of glacial fluor (white limestone sand eroded by the glaciers) indicate the locations of the ancient lakes.

This is an ever changing landscape. Frequent landsides and wash-outs either block or widen rivers. Attempts are made each year to restore paths after winter damage, but when deterioration becomes irreparable, paths may be closed or diverted.

Plants

The overwhelming determinant of plantlife found along the Adlerweg is altitude, particularly the tree line. This, the altitude beyond which trees cannot survive, is found around 1800m on north facing slopes, but can reach nearly 2000m at favoured south facing locations. At lower altitudes, up to approx 1400m, mixed forests dominate with broadleaf deciduous trees like beech and oak growing alongside conifers. Woodland flowers and berries, particularly wild raspberries, grow in clearings between the trees. A wide range of edible fungi is in evidence, and local residents can often be found collecting them for the kitchen.

As altitude increases, so mixed forest gives way to coniferous forest with spruce, pine, fir, juniper and larch all in evidence. Of note is *zirbe*, a fir with candelabra shaped branches, the smooth wood of which is favoured for woodcarving and vernacular furniture. Zirbe grows close to the tree line, particularly on the upper north slopes of Patscherkofel where it gives its name to Zirbenweg (Stage 13). Just below the tree line, full-grown trees give way to dwarf conifers (*krummholz*), which grow sideways rather than upwards.

The high meadow above the tree line is the alpine zone, rich with alpine flowers. Of particular note, and easy to spot are blue harebells (campanula). Slightly rarer are vivid blue trumpet gentians and the pink flowered evergreen shrub, *alpenrose*. Most renowned, but rarest of all, is the white edelweiss. Above this zone, where lingering snow often covers sparse grass on thin soil and bare rock, you can find bright pink flower cushions of rock jasmine and various lichen and mosses.

Harebell (Campanula)

Edelweiss (photo: Christine Gordon)

Wildlife

A wide variety of birds, mammals, reptiles and insects are found along the Adlerweg. Many of these, including foxes, red squirrels, hares and roe deer, can be found in Britain, but there are three mammals that particularly epitomise the high alpine environment.

Grassy higher slopes with rocky outcrops are marmot country. These large rodents are instantly recognisable by the piercing 'wolf-whistle' warning calls of the adult males. Living as family groups in burrows 3m deep, they eat plant greenery, growing to a maximum weight of 6kg by late September. They hibernate beneath the snows, living off their body fat, until they re-emerge much slimmed down in April. Marmots are found at many places along the route, and sightings are guaranteed.

The second most likely high mountain mammal to be seen is the chamois (*gams*). These timid, skittish creatures of the antelope family inhabit barely accessible high slopes where they move with amazing sure-footedness. They are often heard before they are seen, as they run across the slopes generating a rocky clatter from falling scree. Fully grown they reach just 75cm in height and have short straightish horns that hook backwards towards the tip. They live in groups of up to thirty individuals, mostly females and juveniles, with older males living a solitary life.

The ibex (*steinbock*), a herbivorous member of the goat family, is the

The eponymous zirbe (pine) growing alongside Zirbenweg (Stage 13)

largest of the three mountain mammals. Males grow to 1m with large backward facing horns, while females are about half this size. Days are spent on rocky slopes above the tree line where they are safe from predators. In late afternoon, they descend to feed on leaves and shrubs in the forest, where they can sometimes be seen standing on their hind legs to reach juicy higher leaves. Ibex were severely depleted by hunting, but numbers are now increasing.

Black alpine choughs (*alpendohle*) with yellow beaks and red legs are ubiquitous birds, performing aerial acrobatics over the mountaintops. Pairing for life, they nest on rocky cliff ledges at a higher altitude than any other bird species. Seemingly unafraid of humans, they will often try to plunder your lunchtime sandwiches.

The only way to be sure to see a golden eagle (*adler*) is to visit Innsbruck Alpen zoo (Stage 12), where a rather sad looking captive pair inhabit a large aviary. There are 12 pairs living in Karwendelgebirge, although if you are lucky enough to see one in the wild it is unlikely to be more than a mere dot high in the sky. They are ferocious predators with a wingspan of 2m and powerful talons that can sieze creatures as large as small roe deer.

WHAT TO TAKE
Clothing
On a two or three week traverse of the Adlerweg it is necessary to plan for a wide range of climatic conditions, and dress accordingly. But remember, you have to carry everything on your back and weight is at a premium (a good maxim is 'one to wear, one to wash'). The best way to cope with this is to carry multiple thin layers: T-shirt, short sleeve shirt, long sleeve shirt, rollneck, sweater or fleece, underwear, shorts, lightweight long trousers, plus waterproof jacket and overtrousers to protect against wind and rain. Two good pairs of walking socks plus lining socks are essential. All of this clothing should be capable of washing en route, and a small tube or bottle of travel wash is useful. Drying can be achieved overnight (most refuges have drying rooms), or hung to dry on your backpack next day (take a few large safety pins). Accessories should include a sun hat for hot days, and a woolly hat and lightweight gloves for cold ones.

The going underfoot is usually dry and a good pair of summer lightweight walking boots should suffice. Boots should be 'worn-in' but with good tread depth to provide grip on slippery rocks, scree slopes and late season snow. Most refuges provide slippers, as boots are prohibited in sleeping accommodation, but trainers are useful when overnighting elsewhere.

Equipment
A good quality waterproof backpack is essential. Maximum size should be 40 litre (60 litre in the unlikely event

43

you choose to carry camping gear). No matter how waterproof the pack, persistent rain always finds a way through, but a thick plastic inner liner, such as a rubble sack available from builders' merchants, will prevent the contents from getting wet. Anything carried in side or top pockets should be waterproofed with individual plastic freezer bags.

Almost every walker nowadays carries one or two telescopic walking poles. These are particularly useful on steep descents and on unstable ground such as scree. In early season, before mid-July on the highest stages, you may wish to carry crampons and an ice-axe. For the Lechtaler Alpen Hohenweg, karabiners might be useful, but are not essential.

Good quality sunglasses protect your eyes against the glare from areas of exposed white limestone and snowfields, while a high factor suncream protects exposed skin from strong UV radiation at higher altitudes. Although the Adlerweg is not a high-risk area for insect bites, insect repellent is useful to protect against the normal range of insect predators and soothing lotion for post bite relief.

For nights in AV refuges, you will need a sleeping sheet. By far the best, although expensive, is a lightweight silk sleeping bag weighing only a few grams and packing into a bag smaller than a pair of socks. You will also need a towel and the usual range of toiletries. A small torch can be useful at night in a crowded dormitory.

En route you will need a compass, guidebook and a range of maps (ideally with a map case to carry them in). On lower stages, drinking water from springs and fountains is frequently available. However once above 1500m, ground water becomes scarce and you will need to carry a water bottle. For personal health and safety, you should carry a simple first aid kit and a whistle.

SAFE WALKING

Weather

Austria has a continental climate, typified by warm dry summers and cold winters. However, in the western part of the country including Tyrol, this is moderated by both Atlantic and Mediterranean weather systems. As a result, while summer in Tyrol is generally warmer and drier than Britain, the east–west barrier formed by the Alps has a pronounced climatic effect. W or NW winds can bring cool damp Atlantic air masses to the region where clouds may form over the northern slopes. As a result, the Germany-facing north side of the mountains is cooler and wetter than the south facing Inn valley side. Occasional S winds from the Mediterranean bring warm, dry weather, including the well-known Fohn wind. This wind, originating in the Sahara, can cause temperatures to rise 10°C above normal and is said to cause irritability and headaches.

Anchored rubber and wooden steps provide a secure route up the screes of Stempelreisen to Stempeljoch col (Stage 12)

Being in a mountainous region, Tyrolean weather can change greatly from day to day and even within a day. Showers can occur at any time, while heavy thunderstorms are more likely in the evenings. Weather also changes with altitude. Even in mid-summer, rain can sometimes fall as sleet or snow above 2000m.

Summer sun can be strong in Tyrol, particularly at altitude, and can even burn through light cloud. An adequate level of sun protection is essential for exposed skin, and a sun hat should be worn. Lip salve can protect lips from both sun and wind.

Most refuges, and some guesthouses and hotels, provide daily internet mountain weather forecasts obtained from the local tourist office. These are usually displayed the evening before, and are generally reliable. Austrian mountain weather forecasts from ORF (Austrian state broadcaster) can be found at www.wetter.orf.at/bwx.

Mountain safety

Care is always necessary when mountain walking and the Adlerweg is no exception. However apart from the Lechtaler Alpen Hohenweg stages, the going should prove straightforward with few obstacles. The most common safety threat is from slippery rocks, particularly after rainfall, however most places where such rocks occur are protected with precautionary fixed cables. After a heavy winter, snow can remain all year in some higher parts of Karwendelgebirge and Lechtaler Alpen, and fresh snow is not unknown even in August.

River Lech is a popular place for rafting and kayaking (Stage 20)

Help required:
raise both arms
above head to
form a 'Y'

Help not required:
raise one arm above
head, extend other
arm downward

Most of the paths are well walked and other walkers are frequently encountered, although one or two stages are less visited. These include the Koglhorndl ridge (Stage 4), upper Rotlechtal (Stage 18) and Krabachtal (Stage 21). Provided you are properly equipped and provisioned, experienced in use of map and compass, fit enough to cover your planned daily route, have up-to-date weather information and knowledge of accident and emergency procedures, you should have no problems even on the more remote stages. Solo walkers should consider letting someone know their planned daily itinerary. AV refuges usually have a register where you can enter your planned route.

Emergencies

If an accident does occur, help can be summoned in a number of ways. Traditionally the international distress call is a series of six blasts on a whistle (or torch flashes after dark) spread over a period of one minute, repeated after one minute's pause. The response is three blasts per minute. To summon help from the air, both arms should be raised above your head in the form of a Y (if help is not required, raise only one arm, keeping the other by your side).

Much of the Adlerweg is covered by mobile phone reception, which combined with GPS technology provides the most effective way of alerting the emergency services. The general emergency number is 112, or you can contact individual services directly. For police call 133, ambulance 144 and for Alpine Rescue (*Bergrettungsdienst*) 140. Alpine Rescue is a voluntary service, and it is normal to make a donation after the event to Bergrettungsdienst funds. The Adlerweg traverses many types of terrain, much of it remote and only accessible on foot. However, apart from the higher parts of Karwendelgebirge and the Lechtaler Alpen, road access for 4wd vehicles is seldom more than a few kilometres away. In areas that are too remote for road access, evacuation is undertaken by helicopter. Emergency helicopter landing places are shown on OeAV 1:25,000 maps.

Should you require hospital treatment, there are a number of first class hospitals with A&E departments spread along the Inn valley, all well equipped for dealing with mountain accidents. Provided you have an EHIC card issued by your home country, medical costs for EU citizens are covered under reciprocal health insurance arrangements, although you may have to pay for an ambulance and claim the cost back through insurance.

Travel insurance policies usually cover mountain walking provided you are not using specialist equipment such as ropes, karabiners or ice-axes, but check the small print. If you are a member of OeAV (recommended), emergency rescue and repatriation costs are covered by their insurance.

ABOUT THIS GUIDE

All 23 stages, plus the easier variants (marked as U stages) and the eight Lechtaler Alpen Hohenweg variants (marked as A stages) are described in full in this guide, including details of all locations where meals, refreshments and/or lodgings are available, plus a few other locations close by. Stages are grouped into sections, each covering a particular geographic area. The abbreviation 'sp' for 'signposted' is used throughout.

Timings are based on an average walker carrying a moderate pack in good weather conditions, walking the stage without stopping. Appendix A provides walking times and distances between intermediate reference points. Taken in conjunction with

Appendix B, which shows suggested schedules and overnight accommodation to walk the Adlerweg in 15 or 21 days, you can plan your own schedule. Remember to allow ample time to reach each night's accommodation. Average speeds required to meet these timings range from less than 1kph in difficult terrain to between 4 and 5kph on flat country roads. Grades of difficulty are taken from those published by local tourist bodies.

Published altitudes can vary. This guide uses altitudes as they appear on OeAV maps. These may differ from those found on the outside of refuges, which may reflect earlier measurements before accurate satellite mapping became available.

In the descriptions of refuge facilities, the total number of permanent summer beds is shown, with an indication of how many are in bedrooms (b) and in dormitories (d). Details of facilities available and opening and closing times were correct at the time of going to press, but will change over time.

Even the path is subject to change. Rock falls and washouts cause blockages and diversions, some of which become permanent. Look out for local signage showing such changes.

Most geographic features incorporate in their names the German term describing them, for example Achensee (Achen lake), Lechtal (Lech valley) and Loreascharte (Lorea notch). In this guide the full German

The chalet of Schermsteinalm nestles beneath cliffs SW of Sagzahn

name is used with the English description added, hence Achensee lake, Lechtal valley and Loreascharte notch, except on the maps, where the German usage appears.

Mapping is on a scale of 1:100,000. There are 12 maps (indicated on the overview map on pages 8–9), each covering a specific geographic area through which the Adlerweg passes. The main route is covered by 10 maps, plus one showing the variant stages avoiding Karwendel and one showing the Lechtaler Alpen Hohenweg. It is not possible to walk the route relying solely on the maps in this book and accurate detailed maps should be carried. The colours used for each stage reflect the published grade of difficulty. Orange is used for wanderweg (white paths), red for roter bergweg (red paths) and blue for schwarzer bergweg (black paths). Yellow is used for sections using public transport. The abbreviation 'ph' denotes 'pasture hut'.

SECTION 1

KAISERGEBIRGE

STAGE 1

St Johann in Tirol to Gaudeamushutte

Start	St Johann in Tirol (Rummlerhof; 780m)
Finish	Gaudeamushutte (1263m)
Distance	9km
Ascent	900m
Descent	450m
Grade	Red
Time	4hrs 30mins (plus 45min walk-in from St Johann station)
Highest point	Baumgartenkopfl (1545m)
Maps	AV8 (1:25,000)
	FB301 (1:50,000)
	K09 (1:50,000)

A quiet country road leads to a forest path climbing through the Niederkaiser foothills to Diebsofen cave and Schleierwasserfall, where the 60m sheer rock face behind the waterfall is popular with climbers. Emerging above the trees, you get your first close-up views of the jagged Wilderkaiser peaks. The path crosses the heads of two valleys to reach its highest point at Baumgartenkopfl, before descending steeply to Gaudeamushutte with spectacular views of Ellmauer Halt (2344m).

See map on pp52–53

From **St. Johann railway station** (670m), go straight ahead along Bahnhofstrasse, passing the hospital L. Bear L at a roundabout, still following Bahnhofstrasse, to reach the town square, Hauptplatz, with the parish church R. Cross the square and exit far L opposite the post office. This short street leads to Kaiserstrasse where you turn R (if you turn L the tourist office is second building L). Continue along Kaiserstrasse, crossing the Kitzbuheler Ache river. Bear R at a fork (sp Hinterkaiserweg), passing

ST JOHANN IN TIROL, KITZBUHEL'S LESS WELL KNOWN NEIGHBOUR

Situated in the Leukental valley between the Kitzbuheler Alps and the Kaisergebirge, St Johann in Tirol gets its name from a church built by Catholic missionaries before AD738 dedicated to St John the Baptist (St Johann in German). Copper and silver mines, opened in 1540, ushered in a period of prosperity that lasted until the 18th century. Indeed, in the 17th century the 780m Helig-Geist-Schacht (Holy Ghost Shaft) was the deepest mine shaft in the world. Throughout this period, St Johann remained a village, while Kitzbuhel, just 10km along the valley, prospered as a medieval city, its charter having been granted in 1271.

The coming of the railway in 1875 led to the growth of tourism. With extensive development of ski runs in the Kitzbuheler Alpen, Kitzbuhel became one of the most prominent winter sports resorts in Europe. With the Kitzbuheler Horn ski area equally accessible from both places, St Johann shared in this success, becoming a less expensive alternative to glamorous Kitzbuhel. In 1956, St Johann was recognised as a market town and much of the commercial development since has taken place there. The latest census shows the population of the two communities to be almost the same, both having just under 9000 residents.

the bus station R, to reach the main road at a roundabout (10mins). ▶

Note The waymarked Adlerweg starts at the Rummlerhof in Hinterkaiser, 4km from St Johann railway station. It is a straightforward walk through the town and along a quiet country road. As there is no public transport, the only alternative to walking would be to take a taxi!

The wooded Hinterkaiser ridge, cliffs of Niederkaiser and peaks of Wilderkaiser rise above St Johann

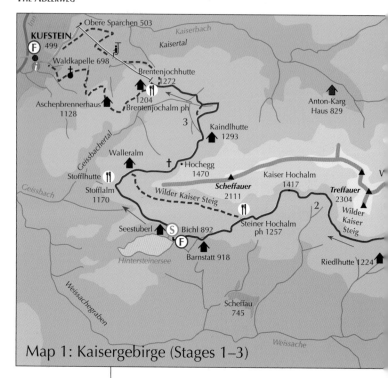

Map 1: Kaisergebirge (Stages 1–3)

Cross the roundabout and leave St Johann by Hinterkaiserweg, which you follow for 3km, ignoring all side roads. The road bends L and R, sometimes quite sharply. Level at first through meadows and occasional houses, it begins to ascend gently as the trees are reached. Looking ahead you can see the Niederkaiser ridge with the bare limestone of the much higher Wilderkaiser rising beyond. Looking back there is a good view of Kitzbuheler Horn rising above St Johann. Shortly before reaching Rummlerhof, cross a cattle grid, where there is a sign L officially marking the start of the Adlerweg. Hinterkaiserweg passes **Rummlerhof** R (780m) (private, no accommodation,

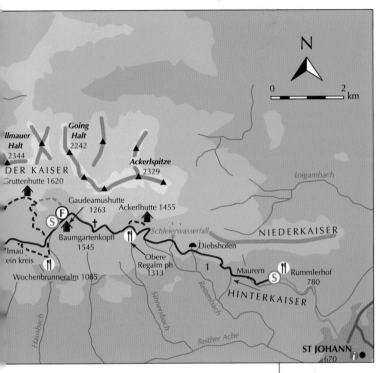

meals/refreshments, closed Monday, tel 05352 63650) (40mins).

From Rummlerhof, continue along Hinterkaiserweg for 750m, turning R to reach **Maurern**, where the road ends. Pass L of both barn and farmhouse on a grassy path, and start ascending through meadows towards the woods (sp Schleierwasserfall). Cross a stile and continue winding up through the trees. After a second stile, drop down L to cross a stream by a wooden bridge and join a 4wd track. Turn R and continue uphill to go straight across a forestry road at a sharp bend. At a second forestry road turn L, and after 100m R onto a smaller forestry road. When this ends, turn R uphill on a path through the trees.

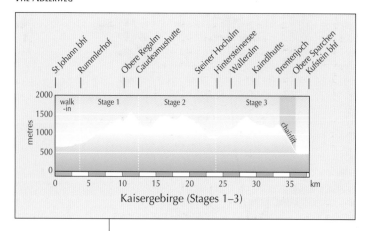

Kaisergebirge (Stages 1–3)

Climber behind
Schleierwasserfall

At a path junction, bear L and contour for 1.5km, with a short section along a cliff face where a steep drop-off has fixed cables for security, to reach **Diebsofen** cave (90mins).

You are now below steep cliffs with a huge open-fronted cavern eroded into them. Follow the path as it

descends for a short way through the cavern. Above your head, the cavern roof is one of Europe's most difficult 'dry tool' climbing pitches. Hanging from the roof you can see many pitons and karabiners left by previous visitors.

Continuing below the line of cliffs, you soon hear the sound of rushing water and a short ascent brings you to the impressive **Schleierwasserfall**. The water tumbles down cliffs with a 60m drop, the path running through the eroded cavern behind the falls. This is another favourite climbing location and climbers are often seen inching their way up the precarious cliffs behind and beside the falls (30mins).

From the falls, continue on the path below the cliffs (sp Gaudeamushutte) for a further 750m, then descend into a coomb. At the bottom of the coomb bear L then turn sharply R (sp Ackerlhutte) and ascend the other side to reach meadows above the cliffs. From here, the jagged peaks of Ackerlspitze (2329m) and its neighbours come into view ahead. Continue through meadows ascending in a long arc, curving round from initially heading NE and ending up heading SW, to reach the top of a ridge at Ackerlrucken.

From Ackerlrucken, an easy walk along a grassy ridge takes you to **Ackerlhutte** (1455m), which can be seen R about 400m away and 100m above (OeAV, 15 beds 0b/15d, self catering, warden weekends only, AV key required at other times) (15mins).

The path descends into another grassy coomb, with the path contouring around to reach **Obere Regalm** pasture hut (1313m) (private, no accommodation, meals/refreshments, open Wednesday/Saturday/Sunday, 1000–1700, tel 06641 309164) (1hr).

Leave by a faint path ascending through meadows behind the refuge (sp Gaudeamushutte), following waymarks painted on occasional rocks. Turn sharp R and continue ascending NW through a coomb to reach a junction with a path coming directly from Ackerlhutte. ▶

OeAV and Kompass both wrongly show the Adlerweg ascending W out of the coomb through dwarf conifers, to head directly to Baumgartenkopfl.

Turn L and contour to reach the day's high point (1545m) below **Baumgartenkopfl**, with a summit cross above the path L (45mins).

Descend slowly on a path winding through dwarf conifers past Freiberghaus, where a magnificent view appears. On a ridge across the valley is Gruttenhutte, and towering above it the spires and peaks of Ellmauer Halt (2344m), the highest point in the Kaisergebirge. Descend steeply into the valley zigzagging through the trees, before bearing L to reach **Gaudeamushutte** (1263m) (DAV, 54 beds 30b/24d, meals/refreshments, mid-May to mid-October, tel 05358 2262) (40mins).

DER KAISERGEBIRGE: THE CLIMBERS' MOUNTAINS

The mountains north and south of St Johann could not be more different. The Kitzbuheler Alpen, seen to the left throughout the first two stages, are rounded and green, and as the site of one of Europe's finest skiing areas are well developed. The Kaisergebirge, towering above on your right, are jagged, rocky and white, and contain many challenging climbing routes and *klettersteig*. Tourist infrastructure is limited to a few mountain refuges.

This difference in development lies in a referendum held in 1961 that resulted in the Kaisergebirge being declared a protected area. Plans to develop the skiing industry were blocked. As a result, only one man-made up-lift exists in the range, the Kaiserlift chairlift at Brentenjoch, which the Adlerweg uses to descend to Kufstein at the end of Stage 3. The range consists of two mountain blocks, the high, wild and jagged Wilderkaiser (Wild Emperor) and the slightly lower Zahmerkaiser (Tame Emperor), divided by the Kaisertal valley.

The Wilder Kaiser Steig long-distance path loops around the Wilderkaiser on a four-day circuit from Kirchdorf. For most of stages one and two it parallels the Adlerweg, contouring around the mountains at a higher altitude. The WKS is a more challenging route than the Adlerweg with more height gain and some sections of klettersteig.

STAGE 2
Gaudeamushutte to Hintersteinersee

Start	Gaudeamushutte (1263m)
Finish	Hintersteinersee (892m)
Distance	12km
Ascent	475m
Descent	840m
Grade	red
Time	4hrs 45mins
Highest point	Before Kaiser Hochalm (1468m)
Maps	AV8 (1:25,000)
	FB301 (1:50,000)
	K09 (1:50,000)

A mid-level walk on forest and meadow paths contouring well below the Wilderkaiser summits before descending to Hintersteinersee lake, a popular tourist spot where it is possible to cool-off with a refreshing swim. Gruttenhutte sits above the first part of the stage and can be reached as a variant route directly from Gaudeamushutte, rejoining the Adlerweg further along. The views from Gruttenhutte are spectacular and it is the only place on the route where you can see Grossglockner, Austria's highest mountain.

From **Gaudeamushutte** head SW (sp Wochenbrunneralm) on a 4wd track. Cross the Hausbach stream and continue parallel to it for 500m to reach a path junction. Leave the track and fork R (sp Riedlhutte) on a path ascending into the woods. ▶ After 200m, the path reaches Gruttenweg (20mins).

Continue ahead (sp Reidlhutte) on a stony path contouring through trees. At a 4wd track turn L, and after 50m turn R onto another track. This brings you to a meadow where you will find **Ellmau stein kreis**, a new age stone circle on a ley line (20mins).

See map on pp52–53

If you stay on the 4wd track you reach **Wochenbrunneralm** (1085m) (private, no accommodation, meals/refreshments, tel 05358 2180) (15mins).

If you turn L you reach **Riedlhutte** (1224m) (private, 10 beds, meals/ refreshments, May to mid-October, tel 05358 2041) (10mins).

Continue ahead on a path ascending through the meadow and into trees to Riedlcol, emerging on a 4wd track at a hairpin bend. ◄ Turn R (sp Gruttenhutte) and ascend steeply round three hairpin bends. 200m after the third bend, turn L onto a small unmarked path ascending through trees to reach the Wilder Kaiser Steig (WKS). If you miss this path, which is difficult to find, continue on the 4wd track for 400m and turn sharply L up steps onto the WKS (sp Hintersteinersee) (40mins).

From Gaudeamushutte a higher level alternative via Gruttenhutte and the Wilder Kaiser Steig is available. The direct route from Gaudeamushutte to Gruttenhutte is frequently closed by winter rockfalls and spring washouts that can take all summer to clear. Before setting off, check at the refuge if the path is open. If it is, head NNW away from the refuge (sp Gruttenhutte via Klamml) on a path that crosses the river washout (often dry by mid-summer) and ascends through scrub towards the col R of Gruttenkopf. This path gains height as it ascends a valley through dwarf conifers and scrub, with the riverbed L. Cross the river (often dry in summer) in a narrow defile at Klamml, and zigzag up the cliffs ahead. This is where the path is often blocked. At the top, join the path coming up from Wochenbrunneralm and continue ahead to **Gruttenhutte** (1620m) (DAV, 153 beds 48b/105d, meals/refreshments, mid-May to mid-October, tel 05358 2242) (1hr).

If the direct route to Gruttenhutte is closed, take the main route towards Wochenbrunneralm, forking R at a path junction and turning sharp R at Gruttenweg (sp Gruttenhutte). Bear R after 100m to follow the path up through the trees. The path winds as it climbs above the trees into an area of dwarf conifers, scrub and scree with a little scrambling over rough stone. Eventually Gruttenhutte comes into sight above L as the path passes below some masts on top of Gruttenkopf. On the col, the direct route from Gaudeamushutte comes in R and the combined path continues a short distance to the refuge (1hr 30mins).

From Gruttenhutte, rejoin the Adlerweg by using the Wilder Kaiser Steig. This follows the 4wd track that sweeps downhill W from the refuge. After 1.2km fork R, leaving the 4wd track but staying on the WKS, on a path contouring through the trees (sp Hintersteinersee) (30mins).

The WKS, waymarked with yellow paint flashes, undulates gently through dwarf conifers and trees, crossing occasional tongues of scree, round the base of Treffauer (2304m), which rises steeply above the trees R. Pass a faint path R that leads to the summit of Tuxegg. After 2.5km, a path comes in L from the valley below (1hr).

The path curves round to the L with a yellow arrow and painted WKS showing the way uphill. Fixed cables protect a short section leading up onto a ridge. Fork L at a junction, where a path R ascends to the summit of Treffauer, and pass through an area with a number of huge boulders, some the size of a house, which have fallen from the mountains above. Continue through dwarf conifers and scrub, and emerge into meadows at **Kaiser Hochalm** with a group of barns and shepherds' refuges (1417m) (30mins).

Descend across the meadows, picking up a 4wd track to the SW that first bears R and then back L (sp Hintersteinersee). Pass through a gate and enter broad-leaf woodland. After 1km, the 4wd track turns L. At this point continue ahead on a path descending through the trees. This comes out above a new 4wd track. Turn R on a path uphill alongside a fence and L through a gate to

Ellmauer Halt, the highest summit in Kaisergebirge, rises above Gruttenhutte

cross grassy slopes and arrive at **Steiner Hochalm** pasture hut (1257m) (private, no accommodation, light meals/refreshments, open all day) (45mins).

To continue directly to Walleralm, avoiding the descent to Hintersteinersee, you can stay on WKS, which contours through the woods from Steiner Hochalm around the base of Scheffauer. This path rises and falls gently, passing a number of enormous termite mounds, some almost 2m high. Far below, through the trees to the L, you obtain frequent glimpses of Hintersteinersee. Cross a number of scree tongues and washouts, and after 3km start descending steeply through scrub and into meadows to reach **Walleralm**, where accommodation is available (see Stage 3).

Leave Steiner Hochalm past barns (sp Hintersteinersee) and turn L on an eroded path descending steeply SW through trees. Bear L to reach a junction with a little used and badly eroded mule/4wd track. Turn R and follow this track, cutting down between eroded and partially over-grown hairpins as the track descends. The track quality improves and becomes a 4wd track continuing downhill. After a sharp bend L, turn R off the track (sp Barnstatt) past houses and through a car park to reach a surfaced road by St Leonhard Kapelle L and Gasthaus **Barnstatt** (918m) (private, accommodation, meals/refreshments, tel 05358 8113) (45mins).

Turn R and follow the surfaced road for 1km to Bichl, on the shore of **Hintersteinersee** lake (892m), and Gasthof **Seestuberl** (private, accommodation, meals/refreshments, tel 05358 8191) (15mins).

STAGE 3

Hintersteinersee to Kufstein

Start	Hintersteinersee (892m)
Finish	Brentenjochalm (1272m)
Distance	10km
Ascent	750m
Descent	350m
Grade	red
Time	3hrs 15mins (plus 50mins descent by chairlift and walk into Kufstein)
Highest point	Hochegg (1470m)
Maps	AV8 (1:25,000)
	FB301 (1:50,000)
	K09 (1:50,000)

A short stage that ascends through forest on a mixture of paths and vehicular tracks to Walleralm then continues ascending to cross the western tip of Wilderkaiser at Hochegg. Dropping down past the little hamlet at Steinbergalm, you cross a small long-since abandoned ski run and the old chairlift that served it. A vehicular track leads to the top station of the Kaiserlift chairlift, which can be used to reach Kufstein. Alternatively, vehicular tracks continue down into the town.

From **Hintersteinersee** take the track to the R of Seestuberl (sp Walleralm) and follow this uphill. This soon leads R onto a path ascending comfortably through the trees alongside meadows. Bear L and continue ascending through trees to cross a forestry track. After 200m, bear a little R to join a broad forestry track. This track continues ascending, zigzagging slightly. The true path runs to L of, and slightly below, the forestry track, although it is far easier to follow the main track. After a short downhill section, where the true path crosses from L to R of the main track, a clearing in the trees below L reveals barns and meadows at Holzentalalm. Bear R to reach a

See map on pp52–53

path junction where the forestry track turns L downhill (40mins).

Bear R and follow a stony path through the trees. This steepens, with a section that requires a little scrambling over exposed rocks, before emerging through a stile and dropping down into meadows. After 200m, join a 4wd track that comes up from Eiberg. This continues across meadows where the little settlement of Stofflalm comes into view through a gap above the track R. A gentle turn L is followed by a sharp turn R at a path junction (20mins).

Turn R and ascend slightly to reach **Stofflalm** (1170m) and the **Stofflhutte** (private, no accommodation, meals/refreshments, May to October, tel 0664 548 6894). A short distance further is Alpengasthof **Walleralm** (private, 19 beds 19b/0d, booking recommended especially at weekends, meals/refreshments, mid-April to early November, tel 0664 985 8139) (10mins).

From Walleralm follow the path that heads NE across the meadows behind the refuge (sp Kaindlhutte), turning R to head E uphill following a tongue of grass between the trees. A short section in the forest is followed by an ascent through meadows to reach the summit at **Hochegg** (1470m), with a hilltop cross L. The last part before the summit has optional paths. As the main R path is heavily eroded, the longer but easier L route is recommended (45mins).

From Hochegg you can see the tiny village of Steinbergalm ahead, the path descending through meadows to reach it after 1000m. In the village is a beautiful small white church R just before the **Kaindlhutte** (1293m) (private, 47 beds 27b/20d, meals/refreshments, May to end of October, tel 0176 2349 4761) (20mins).

It is possible to follow a well-surfaced vehicular track all the way from Steinbergalm to Kufstein. The Adlerweg however uses the chairlift from Brentenjoch to speed the descent to the Inn Valley. From Kaindlhutte follow the vehicular track NNW. After 500m the track

bends R and heads ENE to cross a ford at the head of
Geissbachtal valley, before turning WNW, contouring
along the side of Gamsberg, and climbing steadily to
reach Brentenjochalm. Looking back the entire bowl of
Geissbachtal can be seen, with the peaks of Scheffauer
towering above.

The detour around the head of Geissbachtal can be avoided by taking a short-
cut which goes straight ahead where the Adlerweg first bends R (sp sesseilbahn),
and drops down across meadows, passing Steinberghutte (bottom station of a
dismantled chairlift from Brentenjoch) to the Geissbachklamm gorge. The path
drops into the gorge, crossing the river by a new bridge then turns sharply L and
ascends to regain the main route. The remains of an old bridge, washed away by
floods, can be seen in the bottom of the gorge.

At Brentenjochalm, pass between the old top station
of the dismantled chairlift R and **Brentenjochalm** pasture
hut (private, light meals/refreshments) L and bear R on a
faint path uphill to the top station of the chairlift, which
can just be seen over the brow (1hr, or 50mins using the
short-cut).

Staying on the vehicular track, and forking immediately R, you will soon reach
the **Weinbergerhaus (Brentenjochhutte)** (1272m) (private, 30 beds 30b/0d,
meals/refreshments, early May to mid-November, tel 05372 65148).

The easiest descent to Kufstein is by the Kaiserlift
chairlift. This is an ancient piece of equipment with sin-
gle wooden seats, upon which the custodian places a
cushion before you sit down. It operates in two stages
with an intermediate station at Duxeralm (May to end
of October, 0900–1630, journey time 20mins). Arrival
in Kufstein is in **Obere Sparchen**, 1.8km NE of the town
centre.

The ancient Kaiserlift connecting Brentenjoch and Kufstein

To reach **Kufstein** town centre, turn L in the car park (sp nach Kufstein) and then R onto Energieweg running parallel with the cliffs. Pass a memorial L to Friedrich List (a 19th-century German economist), and further on the R one to Tyrolean patriot Andreas Hofer. Turn R at the end into Kienbergstrasse. Continue ahead on Georg-Primoserstrasse to reach the city centre at Unterer Stadtplatz where you will find the tourist office L. Kufstein Castle, towering over the town, dominates the view (30mins).

If you prefer to walk down there is a choice of two routes, both using mostly vehicular tracks. The first turns R just before you reach Brentenjochalm and descends through the trees via Duxeralm (897m) and Hinterduxer Hof. Between the top and Duxeralm, two large zigzags (one to the R and one L) can be avoided by following obvious short cuts through the trees. From Duxeralm to Hinterduxer the path follows the ski run (1hr 45mins).

The second option takes the L fork at Brentenjochalm and descends slightly following Panoramaweg to **Aschenbrennerhaus** (1128m) (private, 27 beds, no overnight Sunday and Monday nights, meals/refreshments 0900–1800 closed Monday, tel 05372 62220). It then descends with many zigzags past **Waldkapelle** to arrive in Mitterndorf, a suburb of Kufstein 1km SE of the town centre (1hr 30mins).

Kufstein (499m) (all services. Tourist Office 8 Unterer Stadtplatz Monday to Friday 0830–1230, 1400–1800; Saturday 0900–1200, tel 05372 622070). Wide choice of hotels, guesthouses and restaurants. Rail and bus stations).

Romerhofgasse, a quaint corner of Kufstein

AN UNUSUAL WAR MEMORIAL

At noon every day (and again at 1800 in July/August) the town centre of Kufstein is filled with the sound of organ music. The Heldenorgel (Heroes Organ), built in 1931 in memory of the fallen from the First World War, is installed inside the Burgerturm Tower of Kufstein Castle. With 46 registers, four manuals and 4300 pipes it is the largest organ of its type in the world. Its position just under the roof of the fortress gives unusual resonance that, with favourable wind conditions, can be heard up to 10km away, high in the Wilderkaiser.

Tuning and playing the organ are no mean feats. Owing to its position, it experiences extremes of temperature that are an enormous drawback when it comes to tuning. The keyboard, connected to the organ electronically, is situated in the courtyard 100m from the instrument, giving the organist a significant delay between playing and hearing each note. To make matters even more difficult, the organist is not allowed to practise on the instrument itself.

Every performance ends with the tune *Guten Kameraden* (Good Comrades), a melody that best expresses the significance of this place of remembrance.

Section 2
Brandenberger Alpen and Rofangebirge

STAGE 4
Langkampfen to Buchackeralm

Start	Langkampfen Bahnhof (489m)
Finish	Buchackeralm (1340m)
Distance	11km
Ascent	1350m
Descent	500m
Grade	red (black along the ridge from Koglhorndl to Hundsalmjoch)
Time	5hrs 15mins (4hrs avoiding ridge walk)
Highest point	Koglhorndl (1645m)
Maps	AV (none)
	FB301 and 321 (1:50,000)
	K28 (1:50,000)

Leaving Kufstein Bahnhof by train, it is a 6min journey to Langkampfen, from where the path climbs steeply through forest to the meadows above. Another steep climb follows, through forest to the summit of Koglhorndl. The section along the ridge to Hundsalmjoch is graded difficult because of a descent into a notch that requires some scrambling. This can be avoided by using the parallel 4wd track through Koglalm.

See map on
pp68–69

This stage starts at **Langkampfen** station, 8km from Kufstein, served by hourly local trains between Kufstein and Innsbruck. The journey takes 6mins. Kufstein station is west of the river Inn, over the main bridge (5mins from centre).

Alight at Langkampfen (489m), and take the road at the SW end of the platform. Follow the railway for 200m and turn R into Bahnhofweg across meadows towards the village. Looking up you see a waterfall and a small

white chapel above the village with L the summit of Koglhorndl and the ridge connecting it to Hundsalmjoch. Cross the main road by an underpass and continue into **Unterlangkampfen** village (501m) (shops, bank, accommodation, meals/refreshments) (15mins).

Unterlangkampfen village, starting point for walks in Brandenberger Alpen

Cross the village main street and continue uphill along Windschnurweg (sp Hohlensteinalm) passing a signboard extolling the attractions of the mountains ahead. Bear L, and after passing the last houses, continue ascending on Forststrasse. Pass a forestry track R, and soon after turn R to follow a path, well waymarked by paint flashes on trees, up through the forest (15mins).

This path winds steeply up for 3km always in forest, gaining 700m altitude, and crossing five forestry tracks. Shortly before the second track, is a viewpoint looking out over the Inn valley (20mins).

At the fourth track, the path ahead is not immediately obvious. Turn L and follow the track for 25m to reach a sign where the path turns R uphill. Between the fourth and fifth tracks, you pass a strangely carved tree stump containing a spring (20mins).

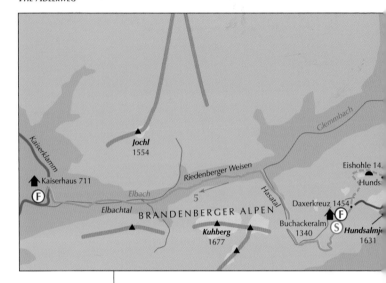

After the fifth track, a wooden handrail aids a short scramble over exposed rocks and tree roots. Shortly before the top, a path comes in L from Niederbreitenbach, after which the trees begin thinning. Continue up through a stile, into meadows (35mins).

Ascend a small grassy ridge, passing a path from Jochalm R, and drop down into the bowl of Hohlensteinalm, a large meadow formed from a dried up lakebed. The path soon reaches **Hohlensteinhaus** (1233m) (private, no accommodation, meals/refreshments, mid-May to late October, tel 05332 56397) (10mins).

The tree covered cliffs overlooking Hohlensteinalm are the flanks of Koglhorndl, and the Adlerweg makes its way up the R flank. A signpost pointing ahead gives alternative Adlerweg routes marked *wanderer* (walker) and *anspruchsvoll* (demanding). The walkers' route avoids the ridge walk between Koglhorndl and Hundsalmjoch by following a path from Hohlenstein to Koglalm and a 4wd track to Hundsalm through a pleasant pastoral valley north of the ridge.

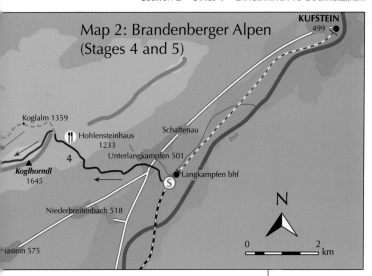

Both routes leave from the rear of the haus, passing the turkey pens L, and bearing L towards trees. At the far side of the meadow, turn sharply R (sp Koglhorndl) on

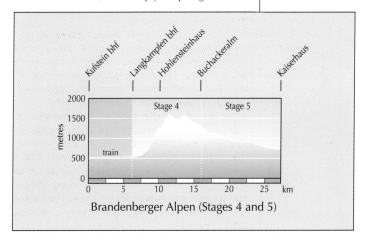

Brandenberger Alpen (Stages 4 and 5)

The notch between Koglhorndl (right) and Hundsalmjoch makes the ridge walk a black stage

a path, waymarked by paint flashes on rocks, ascending steeply N into the forest to reach a path junction (10mins).

The path R is the walkers' route (sp Koglalm/Buchackeralm), which drops down through the woods and across a meadow to a group of barns at **Koglalm**. It then heads SW across more meadows to join a 4wd track running up the valley with Koglhorndl rising L. This track ascends the head of the valley via a series hairpin bends to reach a group of chalets and barns that make up the small settlement of **Hundsalm**. From here, a path R (sp Eishohle) leads across more meadows and climbs up through the woods to reach the Hundsalm *Eishohle cave* (see box). The 4wd track continues ahead to rejoin the main Adlerweg at **Daxerkreuz** (1hr 40mins).

The path L is the main Adlerweg over Koglhorndl and Hundsalmjoch. This zigzags steeply up to a kissing gate where a red arrow shows the way sharply L uphill (15mins).

The path follows the fence L with paint marks on rocks. After 10mins, bear slightly R away from the fence following an indistinct path with occasional paint flashes. The trees thin out and are replaced by dwarf conifers and scrub. The path emerges onto a broad ridge crossing a series of false summits before passing just below the large stainless steel cross on top of **Koglhorndl** (1645m) with a wide panorama of the Inn Valley. Below is the pilgrimage village of Mariastein, with its church, monastery and castle (45mins).

For the next 2km, follow the path (sp Hundsalmjoch) along the ridge, with spectacular views along sheer 800m cliffs dropping down L. There is little or no exposure. Moderate at first, there is a tricky cable-aided descent part way along: this section is rated black. Shortly after the summit, a path junction R gives a final opportunity to drop down to the 4wd track along the valley, avoiding this section. After 600m the path turns briefly away from the ridge, dropping down to avoid a big step (25mins).

Follow a faint path R marked with occasional paint flashes and soon turn back sharply L (no sp, ignore the path continuing ahead). Regaining the ridge at a lower level, there is a view down a deep cleft L. Pass an old wooden cross and continue dropping down with the summit of Hundsalmjoch rising ahead. Fixed cables aid a steep scramble into a notch, the bottom of which is the low point of the ridge (35mins).

The ascent of Hundsalmjoch is partly aided by more fixed cables. An ancient stone wall runs just below the cliff face, intended to prevent grazing animals from wandering over the cliffs and falling to their deaths. After a false summit, the path reaches **Hundsalmjoch** (1637m) with a modern cross (25mins).

Waymarking on the descent from Hundsalmjoch is poor or non-existent. Continue along the ridge (sp Buchackeralm) for a short distance before bearing R to follow a fence as it descends NW. Do not cross the fence. There is a faint path, but this may prove difficult to locate. As you emerge from the trees, where the gradient steepens, bear slightly R away from the fence and contour

By the Adlerhorst is a turn off R for the Hundsalm Eishohle ice cave (20mins).

across meadows aiming for a gate on the 4wd track below. Turn L along this track to reach a peculiar look-ing two-storey wooden structure at **Daxerkreuz** (1454m). This is the *Adlerhorst* (Eagle's nest), which contains infor-mation and displays related to the Adlerweg (30mins). ◄

The Adlerweg continues ahead along the 4wd track before turning sharply L at a zigzag to reach **Buchackeralm**, where you will find Gasthaus Buchacker (1340m) (private, 12 beds 7b/5d, meals/refreshments, early May to late October, tel 05337 62467) (20mins).

HUNDSALM ICE CAVE

Hundsalm is a popular day hike location, with thousands of people each year coming to visit the ice cave that sits in the forest at 1420m, about 30mins walk from Buchackeralm. A remnant of the last ice age, this is the only combined limestone drip and ice cave in the Tyrol. Inside, where the temperature never exceeds 0°C, there are limestone stalactites and stalag-mites as well as permanent ice features, the most famous of which is said to resemble the head of Christ. The cave drops 40m below ground, where the snow is estimated to be 1400 years old. First discovered in 1920, the cave has been a protected national monument since 1956 and open to visi-tors from 1967, with entry only allowed when accompanied by a guide. To maintain a period ambience visitors are provided with calcium carbide torches. In 1984, a previously unknown extension was opened up, and it is possible that other parts of the cave system are still awaiting discovery. (Open mid-May to end of September Saturday/Sunday 1000–1600, mid-July to late August daily. Warm clothing recommended).

Hundsalm Eishohle cave is a 20min walk from the Adlerweg. Visitors are accompanied inside by a guide

STAGE 5
Buchackeralm to Kaiserhaus

Start	Buchackeralm (1340m)
Finish	Kaiserhaus (711m)
Distance	12km
Ascent	–
Descent	650m
Grade	white
Time	3hrs
Highest point	Buchackeralm (1340m)
Maps	AV (none)
	FB321 (1:50,000)
	K28 (1:50,000)

Descending almost all the way on forestry tracks, this is one of the easiest stages of the entire route. Just before the end, the Kaiserklamm gorge is worth a short detour.

Follow the 4wd track downhill heading S from **Buchackeralm**, negotiating a series of sweeping bends for 900m, to reach a junction (15mins).

See map on pp68–69

Turn sharply R (sp Kaiserhaus) and continue down another 4wd track through trees to emerge into meadows. The track takes two sharp zigzags, which can easily be shortcut, before heading downhill with the river R. At the end of the meadows, turn R, crossing the river to re-enter the trees and head down the **Hasatal** valley.

Continue descending NNW on a 4wd track for 2km, re-crossing the river about halfway at a pair of hairpin bends. Further down, where the path crosses the river again, look out for a faint path L. ▶ Take this (sp Kaiserhaus), descending parallel with the track but on the opposite side of the river. At the end, turn L onto another 4wd track in the valley below. Bear R to reach a junction of four tracks (Holzerhutte) (1hr).

If you miss this path, stay on the track round a bend R, then continue for 200m to another 4wd track and turn sharp L, dropping down into the valley below.

Loggers' walkway through the Kaiserklamm gorge

Turn L, (sp Kaiserhaus) ascending a little to reach the watershed after **Riedenberger Wiesen** meadow. This track carries the Vital route, a mountain bike trail through the Tyrol, and is also used by logging trucks. Continue downhill along **Ellbachtal** valley for a further 6.5km. Always stay on the main track, which crosses the steadily widening river three times. After the third bridge, follow the track as it bears R away from the river, to reach a bridge over the much bigger Brandenberger Ache river. At the far end of the bridge R is the entrance to **Kaiserklamm** gorge with a path running through above the river (1hr 35mins).

Once over the bridge, turn L to reach **Kaiserhaus** (711m). During the day, this is a popular tourist spot, which can be reached easily by road from the Inn Valley, but is quieter once the day visitors have left (private, 33 beds 16b/17d, meals until 1800 (Saturday/Sunday 1900), Easter to start of November, bus to Kramsach, tel 05331 5271) (10mins).

KAISER FRANZ JOSEPH I SLEPT HERE

Since the 15th century, timber and hunting have been two of the principal means of income in the Brandenberger Alpen. The trees, once felled and cut into logs, were floated down the torrential Brandenberger Ache river from the forests to the foundries at Kramsach and Brixlegg. Flumes and splash dams were built to help move the logs down river. Most spectacular was the log drive through what is nowadays the Kaiserklamm gorge where walkways were cut into the limestone to give access for the log men. The log drives ceased in 1966, since when timber has been transported by road. The river has been given over to kayaks and white water rafts.

The 500-year-old inn at the entrance to the gorge was an overnight stopping place for Kaiser (Emperor) Franz Joseph I (1830–1916) when hunting in the Brandenberg forests. He was especially impressed by the sight of the log drives, and the name of the gorge and the inn were changed to reflect this royal patronage. The room used by the Emperor and his wife Sisi, is kept in its original condition.

Kaiserhaus, a favourite spot for Kaiser Franz Joseph and his wife Sisi

The crossing of Rofangebirge, between Kaiserhaus in the Brandenberger Ache river valley and Mauritzalm overlooking Achensee, includes a steep cable-aided ascent of the E face of Rofanspitze. While not unduly difficult, this can be slippery in wet weather. An alternative route exists via Bayreutherhutte. Moreover there is a short cut between Kaiserhaus and Zireinersee avoiding the mostly surfaced route via Steinberg. The best route across Rofangebirge is probably to take the short cut route (Stage U6) as far as Zireinersee and then (time and weather permitting) continue over Rofanspitze to Mauritzalm (Stage 7).

STAGE 6
Kaiserhaus to Steinberg am Rofan

Start	Kaiserhaus (711m)
Finish	Waldhausl Inn, Steinberg am Rofan (1000m)
Distance	13km
Ascent	400m
Descent	100m
Grade	white
Time	3hrs 15mins
Highest point	Between Aussersteinberg and Vordersteinberg (1082m)
Maps	AV6 (from Hinterberg) (1:25,000)
	FB321 (1:50,000)
	K28 (1:50,000)

An easy stage mostly on quiet country roads, climbing gently and contouring through the woods high above the Steinberger Ache river, with beautiful views of the valley below.

See map on pp78–79 Leave **Kaiserhaus** SW along the dirt vehicular access road, which becomes surfaced after the first junction. The **Brandenberger Ache** river appears L, with many picnic places between road and river. After 2km, the road turns sharply L uphill, then R. Just after the second bend, turn sharp R (sp Steinberg) continuing uphill on a surfaced road (35mins).

Follow this road uphill through a meadow towards the forest. After 400m fork L, and continue uphill. At the top of the hill, turn L. Soon after **Reischer** farm, the road bears L and after reaching the trees becomes a dirt road, winding through the trees high above the **Steinberger Ache** river. The overall gradient is slightly uphill, with rises and falls to cross a number of small side valleys. After 3.4km pass **Gang** farm L, with a brief surfaced section, then back to dirt (1hr 10mins).

Continue for 1.2km to reach asphalt again at **Hinterberg**. After a sharp bend R, stay on asphalt, taking the upper R fork through **Aussersteinberg**. Distant views begin to open out of Rofangebirge above the head of the valley R. The road continues to climb to reach a summit (1082m) (1hr).

There is now a good view of Steinberg am Rofan, spread out across the meadows on the opposite side of the gorge below, with the pretty white church of St Lambert standing out. Descend to reach the start of the village at Vordersteinberg. Soon after Vordersteinberg,

Panorama of Rofangebirge, with Rofanspitze on the horizon and Steinberg am Rofan in the valley below

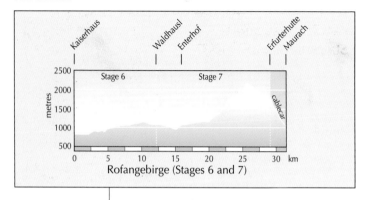

Rofangebirge (Stages 6 and 7)

pass a sharp L turn, which marks the start of the next stage (20mins).

If you are stopping over in Steinberg, this stage continues ahead for 650m to **Waldhausl** Inn (private, 10 beds, meals/refreshments, tel 05248 206) in Unterberg, NW of the village (10mins).

Steinberg am Rofan (1010m) (bank, tourist info Monday/Wednesday/Friday 0800–1200 plus 1430–1700

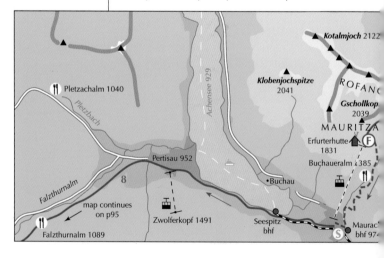

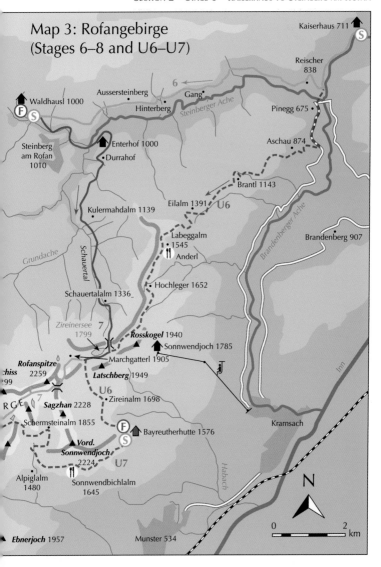

Map 3: Rofangebirge
(Stages 6–8 and U6–U7)

Kaiserhaus 711

Reischer 838

Waldhausl 1000

Aussersteinberg

Gang

Hinterberg

Steinberger Ache

Pinegg 675

Aschau 874

Steinberg am Rofan 1010

Enterhof 1000

Durrahof

Brantl 1143

Kulermahdalm 1139

Eilalm 1391

U6

Labeggalm 1545

Anderl

Brandenberg 907

Brandenberger Ache

Grundache

Schauertal

Hochleger 1652

Schauertalalm 1336

Zireinersee 1799

7

Rosskogel 1940

Sonnwendjoch 1785

Rofanspitze 2259

Marchgatterl 1905

Latschberg 1949

chiss 99

Sagzhan 2228

U6

Zireinalm 1698

RGE

7

Kramsach

Schermsteinalm 1855

Bayreutherhutte 1576

Vord. Sonnwendjoch 2224

U7

Alpiglalm 1480

Sonnwendbichlalm 1645

Habach

Inn

N

Ebnerjoch 1957

Munster 534

0   2 km

Friday only, accommodation, meals/refreshments, bus to Achenkirk), is a small ski resort with a wide range of accommodation. Inside the parish church of St Lambert are two depictions of St Vincent of Saragossa, patron saint of lumberjacks.

STAGE 7

Steinberg am Rofan to Mauritzalm

Start	Waldhausl Inn, Steinberg am Rofan (1000m)
Finish	Erfurterhutte, Mauritzalm (1831m)
Distance	17km
Ascent	1350m
Descent	500m
Grade	black
Time	7hrs 30mins
Highest point	Rofanspitze (2259m)
Maps	AV6 (1:25,000)
	FB321 (1:50,000)
	K28 (1:50,000)

A crossing of the Rofan mountain range, approached via Schauertal valley, and a stiff climb to the mountain-enclosed Zireinersee lake. The ascent of Rofanspitze, aided by cables, is graded difficult. The descent over high alpine pastures to Mauritzalm, by contrast, is easy.

See map on
pp78–79

From **Waldhausl** Inn, retrace your route along the sur-faced road to the road junction in Vordersteinberg (10mins). Fork R (sp Schauertal) and descend towards the Muhlbach stream. Cross the stream on a bridge and continue deeper into the gorge with the stream L. Cross back over the stream to reach a bridge over the larger Steinberger Ache river (30mins).

Ignoring turns L and R, continue ahead over this bridge and follow the road, ascending steeply through trees. Turn sharp R, continuing the ascent, to reach **Enterhof** R (1000m) (limited accommodation, light meals) (20mins).

The gradient eases as the road continues to **Durrahof**, where the apshalt ends. There are excellent views of Steinberg church across the valley R. Continue ahead on a good 4wd track. Bear R at a junction and pass through a barrier into the forest. Continue over a bridge as the track contours in and out of the forest. Views R show extensive modern chalet development on the cliffs above the river, S of Hintersteinberg, before the track reaches another junction (35mins).

Fork R along a less well maintained track. Pass through a gate and across pasture below **Kulermahdalm** farm L, with attractive views R into the gorge below. Re-enter forest and fork L, leaving the 4wd track, onto a good level path through cleared forest. Continue around a coomb L where the remains of culverts and a substantial bridge suggest this was previously a wider track. After a short boggy section, rejoin the track, bearing R. After a short distance leave the track, forking L onto a path following painted waymarks steeply up through the trees. Turn R onto a track, to reach another junction after 50m (55mins).

Bear L (sp Zireinersee) along a 4wd track that ends on reaching the river. Continue on a path ascending through trees and following the river. Cross the river on stepping stones, heading for obvious paint flashes on the opposite bank. Ascend a grassy ridge between two branches of the river, eventually dropping down a little to a chalet at Wimmerhutte. Cross the river by stepping stones again and ascend to a path junction at **Schauertalalm** (1336m) (35mins).

Bear R to follow a stony path zigzagging steeply up the head of the valley, gaining 500m in altitude in the next 1km. Emerge from trees into dwarf conifers and scrub, to reach the saddle at Schauertalsattel (1810m) (1hr 20mins).

Bear L around the grassy bowl ahead, keeping above boggy ground on R. **Zireinersee** lake (1799m) soon comes into view R as you bear round to reach a junction

Mystical Zireinersee lake, with Rosskogel behind

with the alternative path (Stage U6) from Kaiserhaus via Aschau (5mins).

Turn R (sp Rofanspitze), passing L of the lake. Avoid more potentially boggy ground near the shore by hugging the side of Latschberg, keeping about 10m above the

WHY YOU SHOULD NOT WEAR JEWELLERY AT ZIREINERSEE

The Zireinersee is an ethereal place, which ancient legends say is filled with golden treasure. Long ago, so the story goes, there lived a beautiful fairy who, under the spell of a dragon, was condemned to live alone beside the lake. She was a kind and gentle, but lonely, fairy who craved the company of passing wanderers and huntsmen. The 'Wife of the Lake', as she was known, fascinated her visitors, who often brought her presents of gold and jewellery. However, the dragon grew jealous of her visitors and ate them after he thought they had brought enough presents. Full of sorrow that she would have no more visitors, the fairy threw all the gold and jewellery into the lake to prevent the dragon from getting it. Even today, visitors are advised not wear gold or jewellery beside Zireinersee for fear of being mugged by the dragon. Furthermore, if a visitor tries to kill the dragon, the lake will dry out and the dragon will finally be able to get hold of all the treasure in the lake.

water. This is a popular spot for day visitors, who arrive by chairlift from Kramsach to Sonnwendjoch. The path climbs steeply away beyond the lake, to a path junction, where the main route and alternative path divide. The alternative turns L (sp Bayreutherhutte) avoiding the ascent of Rofanspitze, while the main route continues ahead to a col at **Marchgatterl** (1905m). From here, Rofanspitze looks daunting, with the sheer cliffs and pinnacles of its N face towering above little kidney shaped Hirschlacke lake (40mins).

Bear L (sp Rofanspitze), heading towards the gap between Rofanspitze and Rosskopfl, its rocky eastern outlier. Start ascending, slowly at first, on a rocky path climbing the R side of the gap. This soon steepens, eventually reaching the top of the scree (2100m). A level section follows, contouring on a path below the uppermost cliffs, with occasional steel cables for assistance. The final steep ascent starts with a sharp turn R, where a series of cable-aided sections take you up 90m to the ridge. This can be very slippery when wet (45mins).

At the top, contrasting views open out. Behind, a landscape of rocks and cliffs; ahead, a wide grassy bowl, ringed by the gentle rear slopes of the Rofanbirge peaks; to the S, Sagzhan (2228m) and Vorderes Sonnwendjoch (2224m); to the SW, Rofanspitze (2259m); and further away W, Hochiss (2299m).

An easy detour takes you over the summit of **Rofanspitze**. Turn R along the ridge for a short distance, following it round L to take a grassy path along the cliff top to the summit. From here, Erfurterhutte is visible in the distance. The Adlerweg is regained further down, by following an obvious heavily eroded path heading SW.

The Adlerweg turns L along the ridge, heading S to the low point at Schaftsteigsattel (2174m), where it turns R (sp Erfurterhutte) to contour SW, then W, around the grassy lower slopes of Rofanspitze. The route over the summit rejoins above Grubasee lake L. Continue down a broad and often eroded path through Gruba bowl, passing between Rosskopf R and the small Grubalacke lake L. The

The Airrofan cableway descends at 80kph from Gschollkopf to Mauritzalm

alternative route avoiding Rofanspitze (Stage U7) comes in L from Bayreutherhutte (1hr 5mins).

Bear R over a crest, descending more steeply towards Mauritzalm, with Erfurterhutte clearly in view. Shortly before the refuge, you pass under the Airrofan, a unique cableway designed for thrills rather than transportation. Linking Mauritzalm with the Eagles' Nest on Gschollkopf, its passengers are strapped, four at a time, in an open frame facing down. Descending at 80kph, the screams of the riders can be heard far up the valley. The stage ends at Mauritzalm where you will find **Erfurterhutte** (1831m) (DAV, 74 beds 24b/50d, meals/refreshments, end of May to late October, cablecar to Maurach, tel 05243 5517) (30mins).

STAGE U6
Kaiserhaus to Bayreutherhutte

Start	Kaiserhaus (711m)
Finish	Bayreutherhutte (1576m)
Distance	19km
Ascent	1150m
Descent	500m
Grade	red
Time	7hrs 30mins
Highest point	Rosskogelsattel 1868m
Maps	AV6 (from Brantl) (1:25,000)
	FB321 (1:50,000)
	K28 (1:50,000)

This stage provides an alternative more direct route from the Brandenberger Ache valley to the slopes below Rofan. Ascending through forest, the Adlerweg follows a 4wd track high up onto the grassy eastern slopes of Rofangebirge with extensive views back over the villages of the Brandenberg plateau. Continuing on a footpath past Zireinersee lake, it turns south to end below the face of Vorderes Sonnwendjoch.

Leave **Kaiserhaus** SW along the dirt vehicular access road, which becomes surfaced after the first junction. The Brandenberger Ache river appears L, with many picnic places between road and river. After 2.2km, the road turns sharply L uphill, then R. Just after the second bend, the main Adlerweg route Stage 6 turns R uphill (35mins).

The alternative route to Zireinersee lake continues along the road ahead (sp Brandenberg). After two sweeping bends to the R and L, you come to a T-junction with the main Brandenberg to Aschau road in **Pinegg**. Turn R (sp Aschau), crossing the bridge over the Steinberger Ache river, and follow the road ascending steeply towards Aschau. After 1.5km, turn R off this road, continuing

See map on pp78–79

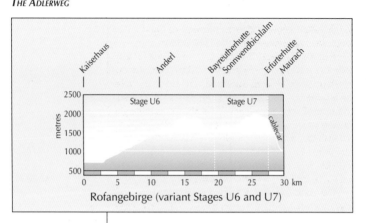

Rofangebirge (variant Stages U6 and U7)

uphill to **Aschau** village (874m) (shop, accommodation, meals, bus service) (45mins).

Follow the road as it winds up through the village. As you leave the settlement, turn R staying on the road as it zigzags above the highest part of the village. The road continues to gain height round a series of hairpin bends. On the apex of the last bend, leave the surfaced road and turn L onto a 4wd track. This is the start of a track that provides access to farms, chalets and holiday cottages, as it ascends steadily for over 7km to Kreuzeinalm Hochleg. Continue through forest, ignoring two turns L, to arrive at the entrance to chalets at **Brantl** (1143m) (1hr 10mins).

Turn R and after 250m reach Wimm farm. Turn sharp L and then bear L ahead to continue on the 4wd track past an old quarry that now serves as a car park for day visitors. The track continues to a gaggle of chalets and barns at **Eilalm** (1391m) (55mins).

Turn sharp L and continue round a series of bends through thinning trees and pasture to reach **Labeggalm**, where you will find the small **Anderl pasture hut** (1545m) (private, no accommodation, meals/refreshments) (40mins).

Leave by the 4wd track, taking the upper route R at a path fork as you leave Labeggalm. Pass a number of old goods lifts L that once served chalets and farms in the valley below and reach the end of the track at Kreuzeinalm **Hochleger** farm (1652m) (35mins).

Pass round behind the barn R, taking a small grassy path that curves up the hillside behind the barn. Follow this through alpine pasture and dwarf conifers as it climbs the hillside S of the farm. Curve around the valley head, and bear SE on a heavily eroded path. You gain height rapidly, with views back across the Brandenberger Ache valley to the villages and meadows of Brandenberg opposite. When you reach the ridge, turn again to head SW, still climbing and follow the path along a broad grassy ridge to reach Rosskogelsattel (1868m).

The path across the large grassy plateau ahead is poorly waymarked. Continue SW, with Rosskogel (1940m) L and the steep spires of Rofan and Sagzahn straight ahead, to arrive at the crest of a ridge with **Zireinersee** lake in view below. Descend this ridge on a well walked path to reach the water meadows surrounding the lake. At this point the route is joined by the main Adlerweg (Stage 7) coming up from Steinberg am Rofan R (1810m) (1hr 20mins).

Looking back from above Labeggalm to the Brandenberg plateau, with Brandenberger Alpen behind (photo: Christine Gordon)

Pass L of the lake, avoiding potentially boggy ground near the shore by hugging the side of Latschberg, keeping about 10m above the water. This is a popular spot for day visitors, who arrive by chairlift from Kramsach. Continue beyond the lake where the path climbs steeply to reach a path junction. Here the main route and the alternative again divide. The alternative turns L while the main route continues ahead to ascend Rofanspitze on a black graded path (25mins).

Turn L (sp Bayreuterhutte) and head S along a wide grassy valley, keeping L to avoid a boggy area. Level at first, the path eventually begins descending with the cliffs of Rofanspitze and Sagzahn rising dramatically R. Bear gently L to pass S of Latschberg and start descending more steeply through rocky meadows with sections of limestone pavement to reach **Zireinalm** farm (1698m) (30mins).

From Zireinalm follow a 4wd track downhill R to a hairpin bend. Just after the apex of the bend leave the track and continue on a path R down steps, through a kissing gate and across a meadow before winding steeply downhill through trees. This path through the woods was very eroded, but path diversions and a series of steps have greatly improved conditions underfoot. A stony path continues descending gently to reach a boulder field

To avoid the scramble up Rofan, the variant route descends towards Zireinalm with Zillertaler Alpen on the horizon

and verdant rain forest below Vorderes Sonnwendjoch. Emerging from the trees through a squeeze stile, ascend gently and cross a boggy area with sections of tree trunks as stepping stones. Bear R to reach Bergalm pasture hut (no accommodation, meals/refreshments) and soon after, **Bayreutherhutte** (1576m) (DAV, 48 beds 20b/28d, meals, June to mid-October, tel 0664 3425103) (40mins).

KARST COUNTRY

The term 'karst' is used to describe landscape where the characteristic features are caused by alkaline limestone rocks being readily dissolved by slightly acidic rainwater. It comes originally from the Slovene word *kras*. The area around Zireinersee contains some of the best Karst geological features found along the Adlerweg. Zireinersee is a karst lake. With no visible outlet, it drains through a series of underground sinkholes feeding springs in the surrounding valleys. The path from Zireinersee to Zireinalm first skirts a dried up karst lake which is kept damp by water bubbling from beneath the surface and later crosses an area of limestone pavement where acidic erosion has weathered an exposed limestone surface into characteristic clints (slabs) and grikes (fissures) so as to resemble paving slabs.

STAGE U7
Bayreutherhutte to Mauritzalm

Start	Bayreutherhutte (1576m)
Finish	Erfurterhutte, Mauritzalm (1831m)
Distance	10km
Ascent	650m
Descent	400m
Grade	red
Time	3hrs 30mins (plus 1hr 30mins walk down to Maurach)
Highest point	Krahnsattel (2002m)
Maps	AV6 (1:25,000)
	FB321 (1:50,000)
	K28 (1:50,000)

This crossing of Rofangebirge is less challenging than the main route over Rofanspitze. The path contours below Vorderes Sonnwendjoch before ascending a 4wd track to Schermsteinalm, which nestles under precipitous cliffs. A final climb over Krahnsattel beneath the cliffs of Haidachstellwand, brings the lofty spires of the Rofangebirge into view, before crossing the Rofan bowl to Mauritzalm. Descend to Maurach by cablecar.

See map on pp78–79

Krahnsattel, with the view north across Gruba bowl to Rosskopf

Leave **Bayreutherhutte** (sp Sonnwendbichlalm) on a path down steps, over a stile, through meadows descending SW towards trees. The path emerges onto a waymarked path contouring below Vorderes Sonnwendjoch through forest with frequent clearings. Pass over a stile in a clearing and cross a boggy area below a spring. Turn R at a path junction, ignoring the path ahead which drops down to Munster. This junction is easy to miss. Continue through a meadow dotted with boulders and cross a stream on a wooden log bridge. The path passes through a gate and ascends gently through meadows to reach **Sonnwendbichlalm** pasture hut (1645m) (private, no

accommodation, meals/refreshments, June to mid-October, tel 06645 321313) (40mins).

Leave past a barn on a 4wd track (sp Rofan uber Schermsteinalm). Continue contouring across open meadows then descend steadily to reach a junction with a 4wd track coming up from the valley below (20mins).

Bear R (sp Erfurterhutte) ascending steadily through a natural bowl towards a col visible above. Pass a barn L and zigzag up the hillside R on a series of sweeping bends. You can see the path ahead contouring across the face of Grubalakenspitze and climbing a notch to Krahnsattel. After the last zigzag, the track continues ascending to join a path that has come from Bayreutherhutte over the summit of Vorderes Sonnwendjoch to reach **Schermsteinalm** chalet (1855m) (1hr).

Just before the chalet, turn L off the 4wd track (sp Krahnsattel) onto a path marked with a red painted sign. Ascend a little, then contour below the face of Grubalackenspitze through rocky meadows filled with a colourful array of alpine flowers and frequent marmot burrows. Cross a number of scree tongues before

Erfurterhutte, Berggasthof Rofan and Rofan cablecar station, with Karwendelgebirge behind, from Grubasteig

Achensee lake from Rofan cablecar – the Adlerweg follows the left lakeshore

bearing R to zigzag up a grassy slope ascending the notch between Grubalackenspitze and Haidachstlellwand. At Krahnsattel col (2002m) pass through a fence and Gruba bowl opens up ahead. The path continues for a short distance to a junction (40mins).

Bear L ahead (sp Erfurterhutte) following the path down grassy slopes with spring-fed Grubalacke lake R and the cliffs of Haidachstellwand L. A slight rise brings you to a junction R with the main Adlerweg route over Rofanspitze (20mins).

From here to Mauritzalm the path is popular with day trippers who have come up from Maurach by cablecar. Continue ahead dropping down on Grubasteig, a wide but eroded path with the complex of buildings at Mauritzalm visible across the meadows, passing under the Airrofan cableway (see Stage 7). The stage ends at Mauritzalm, where you will find **Erfurterhutte** (1831m) (DAV, 74 beds 24b/50d, meals/refreshments, end of May to late October, cablecar to Maurach, tel 05243 5517) (30mins).

Section 3

Karwendelgebirge

Stage 8

Maurach to Lamsenjochhutte

Start	Maurach (974m)
Finish	Lamsenjochhutte (1953m)
Distance	16km
Ascent	1000m
Descent	–
Grade	red
Time	5hrs (plus 1hr 30mins optional descent from Mauritzalm)
Highest point	Lamsenjochhutte (1953m)
Maps	AV5/3 (1:25,000)
	FB321 (1:50,000)
	K26 (1:50,000)

A very easy walk along a valley, with a steep ascent at the end. Descend from Erfurterhutte by the Rofan cablecar (or walk down) and take the lakeside path along Achensee to Pertisau. Continue on a good path through the meadows of Falzthurntal to Gramaialm, and then climb steeply to Lamsenjoch.

You have a choice of ways from Mauritzalm to the start of the stage at Maurach. The 'official' route from Mauritzalm uses the Rofan cablecar from the top station next door to Erfurterhutte (early May to end of October 0830–1700; mid-June to early September 0800–1730, journey time 5mins).

Alternatively, you can walk down following a path starting L of Mauritz chairlift top station (sp Maurach) that winds downhill following a ski run in and out of the trees. Bear R past a junction, passing under the chairlift to reach a 4wd track. Turn L and follow the track down, passing **Buchaueralm** pasture hut (1385m) (private, no accommodation, meals/refreshments, mid-May to late October) (35mins).

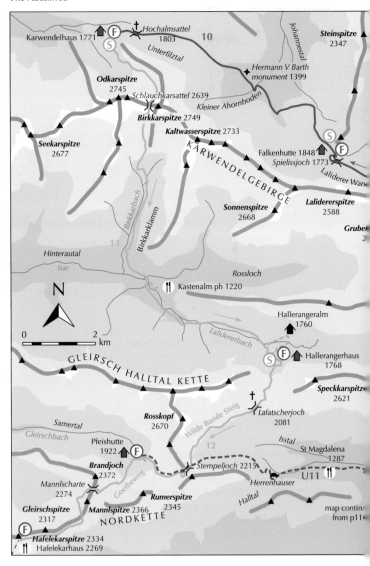

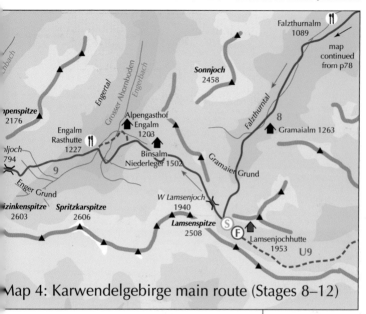

Map 4: Karwendelgebirge main route (Stages 8–12)

Continue around a series of wide zigzags. At the sixth hairpin take another 4wd track R (sp Dalfazalm) then immediately L to follow the path downhill towards the cablecar. This brings you out at the top of Maurach village. Continue downhill bearing R through the car parks to reach the cablecar station (55mins).

Maurach (974m) (tourist office, wide choice of hotels and guest houses, all services, bus to Jenbach, Pertisau, Achenkirk, train (see box) to Jenbach, Seespitz).

An hourly bus service operates from Maurach along the side of Achensee Lake to Pertisau, where it circles the village clockwise. Alighting at Karwendeltaler, near the start of the path along Falzthurntal, you avoid a 5km flat walk.

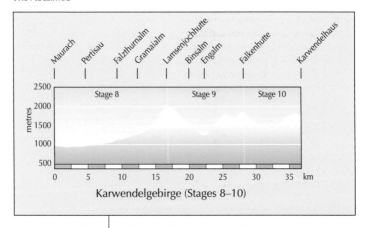

Karwendelgebirge (Stages 8–10)

EUROPE'S OLDEST STEAM COG RAILWAY

It is less than 7km from Jenbach to Seespitz, yet by train it takes 45mins at an average speed of only 9kph. The metre-gauge Achenseebahn railway climbs 440m from the Inn Valley to Achensee with trains hauled by locomotives built in 1888 using a Riggenbach cog system to power them up the hillside. Originally planned as a through route to Bavaria the line never reached beyond the southern end of Achensee.

Over the years, the line has seen boom and bust conditions many times. First threatened with closure in 1927, it was saved when the power company used the line to transport materials for its hydroelectric scheme. During WW2 it had its busiest period, transporting men and materials as an alternative route to the main line through Kufstein. In 1944, it carried nearly 142,000 passengers.

In 1955, the new road from Jenbach to Achensee opened, leading to 25 years of decline and doubt as to the line's future. Then in 1981, the communities around the lake purchased the company and a period of renaissance began. The line is now a flourishing tourist railway carrying thousands of passengers every summer from the Inn Valley to connect with the lake boats at Seespitz. There is even talk of an extension to Gramaialm and on by tunnel to Engalm and Bavaria.

Cross a car park in front of **Maurach** cablecar station, turning L at the road and R to cross the road using an underpass. Continue ahead passing a modern church with a grass roofed parish hall and the tourist office R, to reach the main road. Turn R past a school and local council offices. Cross the road before a roundabout with a central fountain, and keeping some ornamental arches R, descend a short flight of steps to cross the Achenseebahn railway. Turn R onto a surfaced path and descend gently alongside the railway line. After 400m cross the line and main road at a level crossing. Continue for 1km to reach Achensee lake at **Seespitz** bahnhof and landing stage, from where regular boats sail the length of Achensee Lake (25mins).

Continue along the lakeside path towards Pertisau. Pass a small green platform on the lake marking the pipes taking water 5km through the mountains to feed the hydro-electric power station in Jenbach (see box). As you enter Pertisau, turn L (sp Gramaialm) following the road ascending gently away from the lake (30mins).

Keep straight ahead, ignoring various roads and paths R that lead into the village centre. Pass the

Stage 8 is shown as far as **Falzthurnalm** on p78, and continues on pp94–95.

Achensee boat leaving Seespitz

Karwendelbergbahn cablecar L, and bear slightly R along Karwendeltaler to the end of the village (20mins).

Pertisau (952m) (tourist office, wide choice of hotels and guest houses, all services, bus to Maurach, boat to Seespitz (Maurach) and Scholastica (Achenkirk); during peak season, a vintage bus service runs along Falzthurntal to Gramaialm).

THE RIVER THAT CHANGED DIRECTION AND THEN BACK AGAIN

Prior to the last ice age, the river through the valley that now holds the Achensee flowed north to south, running into the Inn at Jenbach. The glaciers changed all that, with the Inn Glacier as it retreated leaving a huge lateral moraine, and the side glacier down Kasbachtal a terminal moraine between Maurach and Eben. This blocked off the river from reaching Jenbach, and Achensee Lake rose behind the moraine. The waters of the lake, not being able to flow south, forced an exit north down Achental and into Bavaria. The river had changed direction.

This situation continued until 1928 when the Tyrolean Water Power Co built a hydroelectric power station in the Inn Valley at Jenbach. In order to obtain feedstock water from Achensee, a tunnel was bored 5km through the mountains under Stanserjoch. Since that time almost all water that leaves Achensee does so by way of this tunnel flowing south, and only a reedy trickle leaves north by the Seeache River through Achental. Man had changed the direction of the river back to its pre ice age orientation.

Continue ahead over a bridge and through a car park and tollbooth for roads to Gernalm and Gramaialm. At the end of the car park, bear L along a surfaced path leading along the broad Falzthurntal Valley. After 2.5km of almost straight walking at first through trees, then through meadows, join a road and continue for 1km to **Falzthurnalm** (1089m) (private, no accommodation, meals/refreshments, open all year, tel 05243 4307) (45mins).

From the refuge, follow the track for 250m and bear R on a surfaced path through meadows. At a washout, the asphalt ends and becomes a 4wd track. At a three-way fork, bear R (sp Gramaialm uber Wiesenweg) following the track across the river. Continuing through a gate and across a washout, the 4wd track becomes a grassy path through meadows parallel to the road. Join this road briefly then just before a gate turn L. Cross the river and join a path through a meadow on the other side to reach **Gramaialm** (1263m) and Alpengasthof Gramai, (private, 36 beds, meals/refreshments, mid-May to end of October, tel 05243 5166) (60mins).

Leave Gramaialm by a gravel track past Franze-hittn (sp Lamsenjoch). Cross the river and begin climbing, to reach a path junction R to Hochleger. From here you can see the path ahead as it zigzags steeply to the col at the head of the valley with Lamsenspitze (2508m) soaring above. You cannot see Lamsenjochhutte, which is hidden until the last minute by a spur L (20mins).

Continue ahead as the path steepens and the gravel track soon becomes a mountain path. A series of short zigzags lead to a long traverse L to R across the mountain. Then another series of zigzags brings you eventually to the col (1hr 30mins).

The Adlerweg zigzags up the screes of Gramaier Grund to reach Lamsenjoch

A signpost points L to the refuge and R to Engalm (the next stage). The final approach to the refuge is confusing. Three routes, all waymarked with paint flashes, wind through the jumble of boulders that make up the col. The shortest route is the middle one, through a narrow gap between two huge boulders, although all three converge at **Lamsenjochhutte** (1953m) (DAV, 114 beds 24b/90d, meals/refreshments, mid-June to mid-October, tel 05244 62063) (10mins).

Before you embark on Stages 9 to 12, a decision needs to be made. Most walkers will want to continue along the main Adlerweg, which crosses the highest parts of Karwendegebirge by the traverse of Birkkarspitze (Stage 11). Indeed, for many this will be the highlight of their trip. However in inclement weather, or if you are struggling with the more difficult parts of the terrain, you may wish to take the easier alternative provided by Stages U9 to U11, rejoining the main route at **Stempeljoch**, shortly before **Pfeishutte**.

STAGE 9

Lamsenjochhutte to Falkenhutte

Start	Lamsenjochhutte (1953m)
Finish	Falkenhutte (1848m)
Distance	11km
Ascent	750m
Descent	850m
Grade	red
Time	4hrs 30min
Highest point	Lamsenjoch (1953m)
Maps	AV5/3 and 5/2 (1:25,000)
	FB321 or 322 (1:50,000)
	K26 (1:50,000)

The first of four high-level stages taking the Adlerweg through the highest part of the Karwendel range. The path drops into Engtal valley, where Grosser Ahornboden is the home to over 2000 alpine maples (some more than 600 years old). It then climbs to traverse Laliderer Reisen below the 1000m rock wall of Laliderer Wande, the highest perpendicular rock wall in the Eastern Alps.

From **Lamsenjochhutte** return to the path junction on the col and follow the path ahead (sp Engalm) to reach W Lamsenjoch col (1940m). Here a view opens out of the north side of Karwendelgebirge, all the way to Birkkarspitze on the horizon (25mins).

See map on pp94–95

Cross a stile and descend to join a 4wd track that zigzags down. Leave the track at the fourth bend on a path L, to short cut the next two bends. Pass a path junction R and recross the 4wd track, continuing on the path to avoid Binsalm Hochleger farm away L. Rejoin the 4wd track, cutting some of the zigzags, to arrive at **Binsalm Niederleger** refuge (1502m) (private, 80 beds 40b/40d, meals/refreshments, mid-May to late October, tel 05245 214) (50mins). Stay on the 4wd track downhill bearing left across the head of Engtal valley.

A path descends R across meadows to **Alpengasthof Engalm** (1203m) (80 beds 80b/0d, meals/refreshments, open all year, tel 05245 231) and the car park at the end of the toll road from Hinterriss. A bus service links Engalm with Lenggries. This valley, although in Austria, can only be reached by road from Germany.

After 1000m turn sharp R to reach **Engalm Rasthutte** (1227m) (private, no accommodation, meals/refreshments, early May to late October, tel 05245 226). The refuge is part of Engalm pasture village, an agricultural area of 510 hectares that is home to over 700 cows and attracts many German day visitors. Looking down the valley you can see **Grosser Ahornboden**, famous for its ancient alpine maple trees (50mins).

ALPINE MAPLES THAT HAVE SURVIVED 600 YEARS

The valleys of Engtal and Johannestal are home to over 2200 alpine maple trees, seen at their best when ablaze with autumn foliage colours. The oldest of these trees have survived for over 600 years, although most date from the early 17th century. Over the years, mudflows from the mountains above have buried the trunks up to 2m deep. This has enabled secondary root systems to develop and aided the trees' hardy resistance to harsh mountain conditions. The wood is almost white, fine grained and, being very hard, has a variety of uses.

In order to protect the trees, Grosser Ahornboden (Greater Maple Land) in Engtal and Kleiner Ahornboden (Lesser Maple Land) in Johannestal have been created *Landschaftsschutzgebiet* (LSG), similar to a British area of special scientific interest (SSI), and a 10 year management scheme is in place. New saplings have been planted to replace trees which are dying of old age. A 'sponsor a tree' scheme is even in place (at €300 per tree) enabling supporters to visit their own tree.

Leave Engalm through a gate (sp Falkenhutte) leading to a path that climbs gently at first and then more steeply, slightly S of W, across meadows with occasional maple trees and stony outcrops, to reach **Hohljoch** saddle (1794m) (1hr 15mins).

Descend briefly on a 4wd track and after the first zig-zag turn L on a path. This path traverses Laliderer Reisen, the scree slopes below **Laliderer Wande** L, the highest perpendicular rock wall in the eastern Alps, which rises 1000m above the valley. After the traverse, a short ascent brings you to **Spielissjoch** saddle (1773m) (1hr).

Turn R and follow a 4wd track up to **Falkenhutte** (1848m) (DAV, 148 beds 28b/120d, meals/refreshments, mid-June to mid-October, tel 05245 245) (10mins).

The route below Laliderer Wande, with Falkenhutte on the grassy ridge and Birrkarspitze behind

STAGE 10

Falkenhutte to Karwendelhaus

Start	Falkenhutte (1848m)
Finish	Karwendelhaus (1771m)
Distance	8km
Ascent	400m
Descent	500m
Grade	red
Time	3hrs 15mins
Highest point	Falkenhutte (1848m)
Maps	AV5/2 (1:25,000)
	FB322 (1:50,000); or FB321 (1:50,000) and 5322 (1:25,000)
	K26 (1:50,000)

A gentle descent to Kleiner Ahornboden followed by a steady climb to Hochalmsattel and Karwendelhaus, with Birkkarspitze, the highest mountain in Karwendelgebirge, rising L.

See map on
pp94–95

From **Falkenhutte** follow a stony path NW (sp Karwendelhaus) downhill across meadows to join the 4wd track descending from the refuge. Follow the track R as it descends through Ladizalm (1571m), continuing to reach a very sharp bend R (45mins).

Take a less used track L ahead through the trees of Saulisswald to reach a path junction (1464m, but wrongly marked 1864m on Kompass). Ignore the faint path L, which is incorrectly signposted as Adlerweg, and bear R to follow the main path NW. After 1km, this path turns sharply L above the washout of a river coming down from the NE face of Birkkarspitze. Stay south of the river before dropping down to cross about 200m upstream. Continue NW into **Kleiner Ahornboden** and turn R over a wooden footbridge to reach the Vital route cycle track. Turn L, briefly joining the cycle track, to reach a crossroads of tracks where you will find a memorial to **Hermann von Barth** (1339m) (1hr).

Hermann von Barth monument, Kleinen Ahornboden

HERMANN VON BARTH, MOUNTAINEERING PIONEER

Hermann von Barth (1845–1876) was a young lawyer from Munich most well known for his exploration of the Karwendelgebirge. His short but intense climbing career started in 1868 in the largely unexplored Berchtesgaden Alpen. By 1869, he had climbed 44 peaks in Allgauer Alpen, including three previously unconquered. In summer 1870, he switched his attention to the Karwendelgebirge and climbed 88 peaks, 12 for the first time, all of them alone. The following year he moved on to the Wetterstein and was the first to climb many peaks there. In 1874, he published his book 'Aus den Nordlichen Kalkalpen' (From the Northern Limestone Alps), in which he documented his experiences and tours, a work still viewed as a classic of Alpine literature. He committed suicide in 1876, deranged by fever, while on a research expedition in Angola.

His name lives on, with refuges, trails and features named after him, including Barthspitze in Karwendelgebirge named in his honour. If you pause for a while at his monument in Kleiner Ahornboden, think ahead to Birkkarspitze, which he was the first to climb, alone, in 1870. You will be climbing this on the next stage!

Looking back from Grasslegerbichl over Kleinen Ahornboden, with Lamsenspitze on the horizon (right)

Go straight ahead at the cross roads (sp Karwendelhaus), along a 4wd track which soon ends and becomes a path. This climbs through the trees, gently at first but becoming steeper as it ascends the meadows along the broad floor of Unterfilztal Valley, to rejoin the cycle track beyond Grasslegerbichl (1749m) (1hr).

At Grasslegerbichl, join a track coming from the R and continue ahead a short distance to reach the cycle track. Follow this easily up to **Hochalmsattel** (1803m) where there is a small cross R (Jochkreuz). Continue over the col, descending slightly to a junction R with the 4wd track coming up from Scharnitz via Karwendeltal. Follow the track curving L, to reach **Karwendelhaus** (1771m) (DAV, 180 beds 45b/135d, meals/refreshments, mid-June to mid-October, tel 05213 5623) (30mins).

STAGE 11
Karwendelhaus to Hallerangerhaus

Start	Karwendelhaus (1771m)
Finish	Hallerangerhaus (1768m)
Distance	13km
Ascent	1550m
Descent	1550m
Grade	black
Time	8hrs
Highest point	Birkkarspitze (2749m)
Maps	AV5/2 (1:25,000)
	FB322 (1:50,000); or 5322 (1:25,000) and 321 (1:50,000)
	K26 (1:50,000)

This, the most challenging stage of the whole walk, with cable aided sections, some scrambling, seasonal snowfields and loose scree, is also one of the most scenic. A steep 900m ascent, straight from the start, takes the path to a col just below Birkkarspitze, from where there is a short detour to the summit. This is followed by a long descent to Birkkarklamm gorge and the pastoral Hinterautal valley. A final easier ascent brings the path to Hallerangeralm.

The path starts ascending steeply immediately outside **Karwendelhaus**. Turn R (sp Birkkarspitze) and climb the steep path winding up through steel avalanche barriers above the refuge. You gain 30m height, aided by steel cables, before coming out on a path across the hillside through dwarf conifers. The summit of Birkkarspitze, topped by a cross, comes into view ahead, and remains in view for almost the whole way up. Ascending steadily, the path crosses some scree tongues before passing two path junctions, the first turning L to Hochalmkreuz, the second R to Odkarspitze (30mins).

Zigzagging up the screes and boulder fields of Schlauchkar marked by paint flashes and occasional

See map on pp94–95

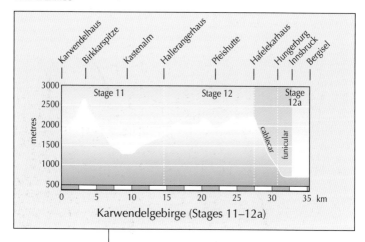

Karwendelgebirge (Stages 11–12a)

cairns, the path crosses a depression where snow may lie all summer. A long steep crossing of scree slopes leads to another series of zigzags scrambling up the rocky lower slopes of Birkkarspitze. More steep scree as the path bears R for a final rocky scramble to reach the **Schlaukarsattel**, 25m W of Birkkar Nothiwak (2639m), an emergency shelter on the ridge between Birkkarspitze and Odkarspitze. (1hr 45mins).

From here, a detour can be made to the summit of **Birkkarspitze** (2749m), the highest point on the Adlerweg. Turn L along the col and scramble up the first (and most difficult) part of the climb. The path zigzags up a few ledges aided by fixed chains passing through a notch with sheer drops either side. More chains take the path over two steps before crossing a sloping terrace to reach the summit cross. The views in all directions are extensive. Zugspitze is seen W, and the Bavarian lakes N. To the S, the Nordkette range blocks views of the Inn Valley, but the high Alps are visible on the horizon beyond (35mins round trip).

The rocky bowl south of the col is an almost perfect example of a glacial cirque. The descent starts down a notch at the west end of the col, marked by a paint flash

The final ascent to Schlauchkarsattel

on rocks (sp Hallerangerhaus). Descend steeply over glaciated rocks, aided by steel cables, to reach the scree 150m below. Cross the scree following paint flashes into the bowl of the cirque where snow may lie all summer, heading S. Continue descending, through a notch in the rim of the cirque, zigzagging down a mixture of scree and steep grassy slopes below. Eventually the path crosses to R of the valley, reaching the tree line where dwarf conifers begin (1900m) (1hr 25mins).

The path turns L and descends steeply to cross the stream in the bottom of **Birkkarklamm** gorge, with more areas where snow may lie all year, some of which are crossed by the path. A long steady descent along the L of the gorge eventually brings the path over the remains of a moraine into **Hinterautal** valley (1hr 15mins).

The valley floor is a complete contrast, flat with large beaches of glacial pebbles and fluor, which has partly buried the trees. Turn L (sp Hallerangerhaus) across the beach to reach a 4wd road. Follow this L to reach the main entrance to **Kastenalm** (20mins).

A short detour takes you to **Kastenalm** pasture hut. Ahead is a private road that cannot be used to reach the hut. Instead bear R, coming shortly to the pedestrian entrance on your L. From here, a path leads through a stile and anticlockwise around the meadows to the hut, with the large spoil tip from a disused lead and zinc mine dominating the view (1220m) (private, no accommodation, meals/refreshments, early June to end of September, tel 0664 5316796) (10mins).

Turn R, or L if coming back from the pasture hut, (sp Hallerangerhaus) to cross a bridge and follow a 4wd track steeply up through the trees following the valley of the Lafatscher brook. Pass a pretty waterfall R, and continue to a path junction at Kohlerwald (1490m) (45mins).

Turn L along a level track, past the faint remains of a disused mine L. Emerge from the trees into a series of pastoral meadows at Lafatscher Niederleger (1580m) where Hallerangerhaus comes into view on the ridge ahead. At Kohleralm (1680m) the track forks (50mins).

Turn L for Gasthof Hallerangeralm or R for Hallerangerhaus (1768m). Gasthof **Hallerangeralm** (private, 80 beds 30b/50d, meals/refreshments, early June to mid-October, tel 05213 5277). **Hallerangerhaus** (DAV, 92 beds 22b/70d, meals/refreshments, end of May to mid-October, tel 05213 5326) (15mins).

STAGE 12
Hallerangerhaus to Hafelekarhaus

Start	Hallerangerhaus (1768m)
Finish	Hafelekarhaus (2269m)
Distance	12km
Ascent	1050m
Descent	550m
Grade	black
Time	5hrs 30mins
Highest point	Mannlscharte (2274m)
Maps	AV5/2 (1:25,000)
	FB321 (1:50,000) and 5322 (1:25,000); or 322 (1:50,000)
	K26

An ascent, followed by a traverse along the Wilde Bande Steig, leads to the challenging ascent of Stempeljoch. Here an aided section (using ropes, planks and rubber steps) often needs renewing after winter damage. From Pfeishutte the route follows the Goetheweg, meandering from side to side of the Nordkette ridge, giving alternate views of Bavaria in Germany north, and the Inn valley south. Descent to Innsbruck is by the Nordkette cablecar and Hungerburgbahn, passing the Alpen zoo.

If you are staying in Gasthof Hallerangeralm, take the path that heads S across the meadows behind the gasthof, crosses the river and ascends through the trees to Hallerangerhaus (10mins).

*Cross on the path before Lafatscherjoch,
looking back to Hallerangeralm*

See map on
pp94–95

From Hallerangerhaus, take the path ascending SW (sp Pfeishutte) through trees opposite the refuge. This soon bears L and ascends steeply a slope of scree and loose rock. At the top, the path bears R, crossing a wooden bridge and continues climbing, on an old mule track cut into the hillside. Continue through sparse grass, dwarf conifers and rocks and pass a cross L. The gradient eases as the summit plateau is reached at **Lafatscherjoch** col (2081m) (1hr).

Turn R following a good track that descends gently high above Isstal valley. At Kohlstatt (1978m), this track turns sharply L descending to the road head at St Magdalena, which is visible down to L (10mins).

Just before this point, turn R and follow a path that contours along the north side of Isstal. This path, the **Wilde Bande Steig**, is followed for 2.2km, crossing occasional scree tongues, gullies, rock outcrops and areas where snow may remain all year, with three sections aided by steel cables. A faint path can be seen ascending the bottom of the valley below the scree and another climbing the scree slope on the opposite side. All three paths converge at the head of the valley.

As the path approaches the scree at the end of the valley it drops down across a rocky slab to a corrie where snow often remains all summer. Crossing this needs care as the area of snow differs in shape and size each year. There are steel cables, but it may be easier to descend onto the scree and pass round the gully. By late season, this snow often erodes to form an impressive snow bridge (1hr 20mins).

The path heads diagonally up across the scree. This whole area is unstable and a system of anchored steps and planks is used to form a path across the slope. Having crossed the slope, the path turns R (joining the path coming up the valley) and zigzags up the L of the scree. More anchored steps and planks, some of which need renewing in spring after winter damage, help you gain height quickly. After a stiff climb, you arrive at **Stempeljoch** col (2215m) (30mins).

Descent from the col is much easier than the ascent. Drop down R on a good track that soon turns sharply back L. After 150m, ignore a path ahead contouring across the scree, and drop down R, into the bowl below the col, on a series of wide sweeping bends. This track continues WSW across a grassy area, eventually curving round to bear NW. Pass a barn L at Pfeisalm and turn L on a 4wd track leading to **Pfeishutte** (1922m) (OeAV, 75 beds 35b/40d, meals/refreshments, end of May to mid-October, tel 0512 292333) (30mins).

From Pfeishutte the Adlerweg follows the **Goetheweg** path, a popular day trip excursion from the Nordkette cablecar. Leaving the refuge SW (sp Hafelekar), the path climbs steadily through grass and dwarf conifers heading for the gap between Rumerspitze and Gleirschtaler Brandjoch. After 1km, turn R and zigzag up the grassy hillside on a good path. At the top, bear L and follow the path across the scree, turning R after 500m. Traverse R and back L to ascend the scree slope. At the top, the path passes through **Mannlscharte** notch (2274m) (50mins).

Zigzag a short way down the N side of the mountain with a section of fixed cable for security. Bear L on a path contouring below Mannlspitze along a series of ledges with fixed cables. At a bend L, a painted sign indicates Zugspitze *blick* where you get a good, if distant, view of Germany's highest mountain. Nearer, you can see ahead the cross and viewpoint on the summit of Hafelekar. Rising again, the path recrosses the ridge at Muhlkarscharte, between Mannlspitze and Gleirschspitze, bringing Innsbruck clearly into view (30mins).

Bearing R, the path contours below Gleirschspitze with handrails for security, after which it closely follows the Nordkette ridge, crossing frequently between south and north of the ridgeline most of the way to Hafelekarhaus, finally passing south below Hafelekarspitze to reach **Hafelekarhaus** (2269m) (private, no accommodation, meals/refreshments, open when cablecar operates) (40mins).

To visit **Hafelekarspitze** (2334m), turn R about 400m before the end and follow a short path that zigzags up to the summit, where there are extensive views in all directions. This path continues over the summit and zigzags down to Hafelekarhaus.

Nordkette cablecar descending from Seegrube to Hungerburg

The Adlerweg uses the Nordkette cablecar to reach **Innsbruck**. This descends in two stages, Hafelekar to Seegrube and Seegrube to Hungerburg. At Hungerburg the journey to Innsbruck city centre can be continued by either bus (route J) or the ultra modern Hungerburgbahn funicular, which crosses the Inn and terminates in an underground station below the conference centre. On the way, it stops at Innsbruck **Alpen zoo** (open daily, all year, 0900–1800) where you can visit the captive golden eagles. A combined ticket for cablecar and funicular can be bought at Hafelekarhaus (cablecar operates late April to early November 0830–1700, subject to weather conditions, 20mins journey).

If you want to walk down to Innsbruck, it is best to leave the Goetheweg at Gleirschjochl, the col between Gleirschspitze and Hafelekarspitze, and follow the waymarked path L (sp Seegrube) first to **Seegrube** (1906m) (1hr) where you join a 4wd track zigzagging down to **Hungerburg** (868m) (2hrs 30mins).

STAGE U9
Lamsenjoch to Vomperberg

Start	Lamsenjochhutte (1953m)
Finish	Karwendelrast inn, Vomperberg (860m)
Distance	13km
Ascent	100m
Descent	1200m
Grade	red
Time	3hrs30min
Highest point	Lamsenjochhutte (1953m)
Maps	AV5/3 (1:25,000)
	FB321 (1:50,000)
	K26 (1:50,000)

The first part of the variant route avoiding the traverse of Birkkarspitze. This stage descends steadily from Lamsenjoch down Stallental valley to reach a roadhead at Barenrast, with views of St Georgenberg monastery in the valley below. It then contours around Vomperjoch, following the Alpsteig path to the eastern end of the agricultural Vomperberg plateau, from where a forest path runs to the Karwendelrast inn.

The paths on the variant route are less popular than those that make up the main Adlerweg through Karwendelgebirge, and waymarking throughout is less well provided than on the main route.

Descend SE from **Lamsenjochhutte** on the 4wd access track. After 100m a faint path, waymarked by occasional paint flashes, forks R and drops into the rocky bowl below the track. This is the official Adlerweg. However,

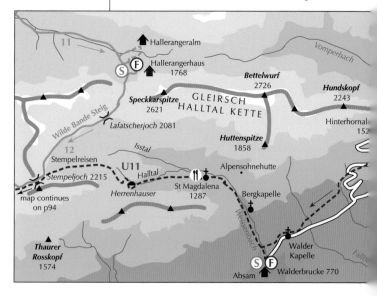

it is poorly marked and it is preferable to stay on the 4wd track. After 1.75km, the two routes come together at Badstube (40mins).

Continue descending along Stallental and drop down a moraine with Stallenhutte in view ahead. The official route bears R at a washout 100m before the refuge and continues with the river L. To reach **Stallenhutte** (1340m), cross the washout and meadow beyond (private, basic accommodation 10 beds 0b/10d, simple meals/refreshments, tel 05353 5228) (35mins).

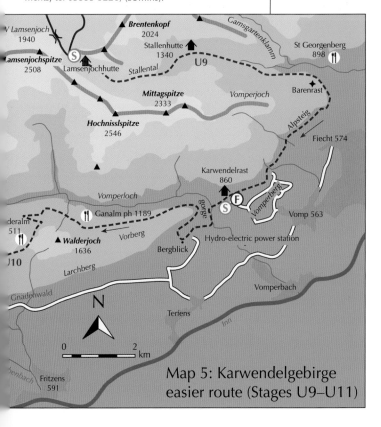

Map 5: Karwendelgebirge easier route (Stages U9–U11)

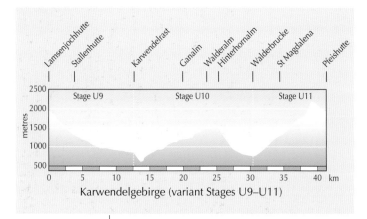

Karwendelgebirge (variant Stages U9–U11)

St Georgenberg monastery perched above Wolfsklamm gorge

Continue down through meadows with impressive glaciated cliffs above L. After the path from the refuge crosses the river washout, the two tracks merge and continue through meadows with occasional trees. Bear L at a track junction, continuing downhill into forest, and L again at the next junction. As the valley deepens, the track runs along a hillside with steep drops L. Pass a

couple of memorial shrines and bear R at the next junction, where a path L drops down to St Georgenberg monastery. Pass a fork R and continue through the barrier and past a car park L to reach **Barenrast** R, where there is a monument to the last bear in North Tyrol, which was killed on 14 May 1898 (55mins).

Memorial to the last bear killed in Tyrol at Barenrast in 1898

Continue past a meadow L and fork R uphill (sp Karwendelrast) along **Alpsteig**. Follow this track as it contours SW around Vomperjoch with views of the old silver mining town of Schwaz through trees below L. After 3.5km, arrive at 4-way path junction. Cross a bridge and bear R steeply uphill to a surfaced road at Alpsteig, overlooking the agricultural plateau of Vomperberg (50mins).

Turn R, then L on a track behind a row of houses. Turn L after the third house, just before the path enters trees. Descend on a faint grassy path alongside a meadow with trees R. Pass behind two farmhouses at Kampfl Eggl, and through a gate ahead onto a 4wd track into trees. This ascends slightly, then descends alongside a meadow to a surfaced road. Turn L and shortly come to Gasthof **Karwendelrast** (860m) (private, 21 beds 13b/8d, meals/refreshments, closed Thursday, tel 05242 62251) (30mins).

THE RICHEST SILVER MINES IN THE WORLD

At the beginning of the 16th century, the Tyrol was the centre of a very successful silver mining industry, producing the purest silver in the world. The industry was centred around the town of Schwaz, at the time the second largest city in Austria. The silver miners were prosperous by medieval standards. This can clearly be seen in Schwaz parish church which has two aisles, one richly decorated by the miners and the other plainer for the rest of the congregation. The most successful mines were controlled by the Fugger family of financiers from Augsburg, who were probably the richest men of their day.

Much of the silver was taken to Hall in Tirol, where the Austrian mint (Munze Hall) produced silver 'Thaler' coins. As these were the purest silver coins in Europe, they were used as a trading currency across the continent. Indeed the name Thaler is regarded by etymologists as the origin of the word Dollar (say it quickly and you will see why).

This prosperity came to an end when the Spanish discovered a lode of pure silver in S America, which could be mined more cheaply than Tyrolean silver. Now all that remains are remote spoil tips and a heritage mine in Schwaz, where tourists can relive the olden days.

STAGE U10
Vomperberg to Absam

Start	Karwendelrast inn, Vomperberg (830m)
Finish	Walderbrucke inn, Absam (770m)
Distance	16km
Ascent	1000m
Descent	1100m
Grade	red
Time	6hrs 30mins
Highest point	Hinterhornalm (1522m)
Maps	AV5/3 and 5/2 (1:25,000)
	FB321 (except last 1km) or 322 (1:50,000)
	K26 (1:50,000)

Cross the Vomper Bach valley and follow the 4wd track climbing along the south side of Vomper Loch canyon, passing two alpine pasture huts to reach high pastures at Hinterhornalm. A path going down through forest shortens many hairpins on the descent above Gnadenwald before cutting through forest to reach the Walderbrucke inn in the village of Absam.

The path goes NW into the trees opposite the back entrance to **Karwendelrast** (sp Kraftwerk (power station)) and heads steeply down bearing L. Cross a 4wd track, continuing steeply down a faint path to reach the river below an intake sluice at the bottom of the gorge. Turn R under an overhanging rock and cross a bridge. Turn L, zig-zagging down to the river and cross back to the east bank at the next bridge. Continue following the river, crossing for the last time at the third bridge, where a sign advises no more than two people should use the bridge at the same time. Just before the fourth bridge, a faint path turns R (15mins).

See map on pp116–117

Footbridge over Vomperbach in the gorge below Karwendelrast

Do not cross the bridge. Follow the path R alongside the river (sp Umlberg) to cross a washout and scree, then ascend some slippery wooden steps at the start of a partly overgrown, steep zigzag path out of the gorge. Emerge onto a 4wd track almost underneath an electricity power line. Turn R then bear round L as the track climbs steeply up Wegstal. Turn L at a forest track junction continuing gently uphill through meadows to reach a surfaced road (1hr).

Turn R uphill, passing houses at **Bergblick** and continue on a 4wd track to cut the corner R at a T-junction. Turn R (sp Ganalm).

You are now on a good quality 4wd track, running 9km to Walderalm. Head NE to a viewpoint over Vomperberg, Schwaz and the lower Inn valley. Here the track continues ahead through a barrier, passing another track heading up the hillside L, to head W above the side of Vomper Loch canyon. Pass a track R leading into the canyon and continue ascending gently to a summit with views down into the canyon and to Ganalm refuge ahead. Descend a little around the head of Gannerklamm with the road cut into the cliff face, to reach **Ganalm** pasture hut, which sits on a promontory 50m R (1189m) (private, no accommodation, meals/refreshments, May to end of October) (1hr 35mins).

From Ganalm to Walderalm the route originally followed a zigzag path L steeply up through the meadow and into trees above. However, a series of washouts and fallen trees have blocked this path and the recommended route now continues along the forestry track (sp Walderalm) gaining height by a series of hairpins. This emerges into high pastures with a chapel L and

Looking down into Vomper Loch canyon from Ganalm pasture hut

Walderalm refuge (1511m) above R (private, no accommodation, meals/refreshments, May to end of October,
tel 05223 48240) (1hr 40mins).

From the cross roads S of the refuge, follow an
excellent quality dirt road ahead, then fork R through
open forest with trees well back from the track, to reach
Hinterhornalm refuge (1524m) (private, no accommodation, meals/refreshments, mid-May to start of November,
tel 0664 2112745) (20mins).

Beyond Hinterhornalm there have been more problems with the original route, which contoured across the
mountainside below Walderkampspitze before dropping
down into Halltal. A major washout has closed this path
and the route now heads more directly to Absam, cutting
through the forest above Gnadenwald. Leave the refuge
by a footpath heading SW (sp Gnadenwald St Martin)
crossing a meadow and zigzagging down through trees.
Bear L at a forest track and continue down to cross a surfaced road. This is the access road to Hinterhornalm and
the path crosses it five times. At the fifth crossing, continue ahead on the path and bear R (sp Absam) to drop
down to cross the Urschenbach river (50mins). The river
crossing is not always easy, as winter floods cause major
washouts and deepening of the gorge. ▶

Cross the river where indicated by signs and turn L
on the opposite bank on a path downhill through trees.
At a junction, continue ahead on a 4wd track descending
gently to reach a point just above a car park at **Walder
Kapelle**. Bear R, then L, contouring above the main
road following Jakobsweg. Just before the track drops
R to cross the river in Halltal, turn L and soon come to
Gasthof **Walderbrucke** (770m) (private, 28 beds 28b/0d,
meals until 2030/refreshments, open all year, closed
Wednesday and Thursday, tel 05223 57916) (50mins).

If the river is
impassable, retrace
your steps to the road
and follow it down
towards Gnadenwald
St Martin. From there
follow the well-signed
Jakobsweg pilgrim
path R to reach
Absam.

STAGE U11
Absam to Pfeishutte

Start	Walderbrucke inn, Absam (770m)
Finish	Pfeishutte (1922m)
Distance	11km
Ascent	1450m
Descent	300m
Grade	red
Time	4hrs
Highest point	Stempeljoch (2215m)
Maps	AV5/2 (1:25,000)
	FB321 (1:50,000) and 5322 (1:25,000); or 322 (1:50,000)
	K26 (1:50,000)

The route follows historic Salzbergstrasse, the toll road ascending Halltal valley, to reach the abandoned salt mines at Herrenhauser, a very atmospheric location. From Issjoch a narrow path traverses scree slopes and climbs to Stempeljoch col. Here it joins Stage 12 for the descent to Pfeishutte.

St Magdalena gasthof and church on Salzbergstrasse, 'the old salt road', in Halltal

The path starts R of **Walderbrucke** inn on a track passing through a barrier and ascending to reach a junction with Jakobsweg. Turn L and drop down to cross the river. Turn R onto Salzbergstrasse heading uphill (sp St Magdalena). This is a surfaced road that for 700 years was used to bring salt down from the mines at Herrenhauser to Hall. ▸ Continue past an ancient chapel at **Bergkapelle** (AD1325), to a point just before the road crosses the river, where there is a path L (25mins).

Follow this path (sp Fluchtsteig) uphill, parallel with the road. Pass over a wooden bridge and round a coomb with fixed cables for security. Continue above a washout on the road below and bear L up the hillside just before a car park. Ascend steeply through trees on a good stony path and across a meadow to reach **St Magdalena**, a church with an old cloister that now holds a restaurant (1287m) (private, no accommodation, meals/refreshments, closed Monday, tel 05223 41420) (55mins).

Leave by the upper of two 4wd tracks rising W into the trees (sp Pfeishutte). Pass over a rise to rejoin Salzbergstrasse. Turn L, ascending past a car park, through a barrier and over a bridge, where the asphalt ends and becomes a 4wd track. Pass the mineshaft of the disused Erzherzogberg mine L, and zigzag up to the old

Stage U11 is shown as far as **Stempeljoch** on p116, and continues on p94.

To avoid using Salzbergstrasse you can walk up Rodelbahn, a toboggan run that descends in the trees parallel to the road L.

Disused salt mine offices and workshops at Herrenhauser on the slopes of Salzberg ('salt mountain')

salt works buildings at **Herrenhauser** (1485m) that are visible on the ridge ahead (30mins).

SALT, THE WHITE GOLD OF HALLTAL

Salt mining at Herrenhauser at the head of Halltal valley commenced in 1272, although archaeological evidence suggests some form of salt extraction may go back to 500bc. By 1555, there was a total length of 20km of tunnels, and when the mines closed in 1967 there were eight tunnel systems totalling 80km of tunnels, with 25km still operational. As of 2010, 7km of tunnels were still accessible. The impressive mine buildings still stand on a crest looking down the valley, although they are now closed. After extraction, the salt was sent through wooden pipes to saltpans around St Magdalena, and then taken down Salzbergstrasse (Salt Mountain Street) for processing in the Saline hall and storage in the salt warehouses of Hall in Tirol. The citizens of Hall regarded salt as 'white gold' and its importance is reflected in the city's coat of arms, which depicts two lions with a saltcellar.

A series of wide zigzags take the track up and across the old mine workings, with spoil heaps and a series of curious domed structures. At the end of the mine, the track bends sharply L and R. At this point, a path turns off L (sp Pfeishutte). Follow this path zigzagging up through the trees to emerge on the scree slopes of Stempelreisen. Contour across the scree rising steadily. Stempeljoch col is visible ahead. Ignore the first faint path up the scree towards the col, continuing at a lower level to join the main Adlerweg path (Stage 12) at the point where it reaches the base of the scree. This is below the col to R (1hr 10mins).

The path heads diagonally up across the scree. This whole area is unstable and a system of anchored steps and planks is used to form a path across the slope. Having crossed the slope, the path turns R and zigzags up the L of the scree. More anchored steps and planks, some of which need renewing in spring after winter damage, help you gain height quickly. After a stiff climb, you arrive at **Stempeljoch** col (2215m) (30mins).

Descent from the col is much easier than the ascent. Drop down R on a good track that soon turns sharply back L. After 150m, ignore a path ahead contouring across the scree, and drop down R, into the bowl below the col, on a series of wide sweeping bends. This track continues WSW across a grassy area, eventually curving round to bear NW. Pass a barn at Pfeisalm L and turn L on a 4wd track leading to **Pfeishutte** (1922m) (OeAV, 75 beds 35b/40d, meals/refreshments, end of May to mid-October, tel 0512 292333) (30mins).

The Karwendel variant climbs across the screes of Stempelreisen above Isstal, to rejoin the Adlerweg at Stempeljoch col

SECTION 4
INNSBRUCK AND PATSCHERKOFEL

STAGE 12A
Innsbruck city tour

Start	Hungerburgbahn base station (569m)
Finish	Bergisel tram terminus (590m)
Distance	2km
Ascent	75m
Descent	–
Grade	white
Time	40min to 2hrs depending upon stops
Highest point	Bergisel (635m)
Maps	AV31/5 (1:50,000)
	FB333 or 322 (1:50,000)

An opportunity to escape the mountains for a few hours and see the main sights of Innsbruck, the Tyrolean capital. This city tour passes places linked to three of the most significant figures in the city's history: Emperor Maximilian, Hapsburg Empress Maria Theresa and Andreas Hofer, local resistance leader against Napoleon.

From the Hungerburgbahn funicular base station under the **Congresshaus**, walk S along Rennweg, with first the **Hofgarten** and then **Landestheater** on L. Along Rennweg you will find *fiacre* plying to take tourists on carriage rides around the city. Pass the **Hofburg** palace R and at the end of Rennweg turn R under an arch. The building immediately ahead, before you turn, is the **Hofkirche**, entry to which is through the **Volkskunst** museum L.

Continue along Hofgasse, a narrow pedestrian alley lined with tourist shops, passing the entrance to Hofburg

R. In the Hofburg palace entrance is a branch of the famous Café Sacher where you could stop for a piece of Sachertorte chocolate cake. The alley leads into a square in front of Maximilian's palace, which was the heart of the medieval city. The old palace is instantly identifiable by the famous **Goldenes Dachl** (golden roof) which covers a viewing balcony overlooking the square. The palace nowadays holds a museum and the city registry office, with wedding groups often celebrating on the steps.

Turn L to head S along Herzog Fredrichstrasse, with the baroque stucco façade of Heblinghaus R. As you leave the narrow streets of the *Altstadt* (old city) you cross Burg Graben/Markt Graben, with tram tracks running along the street. The tourist office is the second building L on Burg Graben (10mins).

Cross the tram tracks and continue ahead along the wide pedestrianised Maria Theresien Strasse. Pass the **Annasaule monument** (commemorating Tyrolean resistance against the Bavarians during the war of Spanish Succession in 1703) and the Altes Landhaus L, which houses the Tyrolean regional

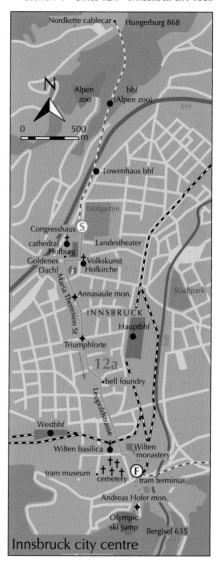

Innsbruck city centre

*The ultra-modern
Hungerburgbahn
funicular connects
Hungerburg with
Innsbruck below,
passing the Alpen zoo*

assembly. At the end of the street is **Triumphforte** arch commemorating the marriage of Leopold II to Maria Ludovica.

Continue ahead into Leopoldstrasse, and follow it for 800m as it bears first L then R, to reach the Wilten district of the city. Pass Grassmayr **bell foundry** and museum L. This 400 year old foundry, which can be visited, is one of the last in Europe where bells are still cast using traditional methods. Continue over the railway bridge and pass **Wilten basilica** R, a pilgrimage church with spectacular stucco and ceiling paintings, much of which has been restored following bomb damage during WW2. Bear L in front of **Wilten monastery** and almost immediately reach the Bergisel tram terminus (30mins).

INNSBRUCK, THE TYROLEAN CAPITAL

The history of Innsbruck is inextricably linked to three significant historical figures, a medieval emperor, a Hapsburg empress and a partisan.

During the reign of the Austrian Archduke and Holy Roman Emperor **Maximilian the First** (1459–1519), the political and strategic importance of the Inn valley was first recognised and Innsbruck became the provincial capital. Maximilian favoured Innsbruck as the location for his second marriage (his first wife, Maria of Burgundy, had died) to Bianca Maria Sforza daughter of the Duke of Milan, and to mark the occasion had the famous *Goldenes Dachl* built onto the front of his palace overlooking the main square. This is a covered balcony decorated with pictures depicting him and his two wives, which allowed the emperor to watch celebrations in the square without getting wet. Maximilian wished to be buried in Innsbruck and commissioned the building of the Hofkirche to hold his sumptuous mausoleum. However this building was never to receive his body, as the burghers, enraged by large debts run up by his court, shut the gates of the city against him. Maximilian died in Upper Austria and was buried in Weiner Neustadt.

Maria Theresa (1717–1780) is often described as the most powerful woman the world has ever seen. The last of the pure Hapsburg rulers, her dominions included Austria, Hungary, Croatia, Bohemia, Silesia, Mantua, Milan, Parma and the Netherlands. Despite her reign being punctuated by a series of foreign wars, she still found time to give birth to 16 children, all but three of whom survived infancy. Maria Theresa's main mark upon Innsbruck is the imperial Hofburg Palace that she had rebuilt between 1754 and 1773 in Baroque style with Rococo details. She particularly favoured Innsbruck as her husband, Emperor Francis Stephan, had spent most of his early life there, and they visited the city frequently. During one of these visits in 1765, they planned to hold the wedding ceremony of their son Leopold to the daughter of the king of Spain. Unfortunately, during the festivities, her husband died of a heart attack and the occasion became one of sadness not joy. The triumphal arch, in Maria Theresien Strasse, depicts this with the south side showing the joy of marriage and the north the sadness of death. Following Francis's death, Maria Theresa withdrew from public life and went into a prolonged period of mourning. In later years, she claimed that her happiness ended in Innsbruck.

Andreas Hofer (1767–1810), a Tyrolean innkeeper, came to prominence in 1809 when he led a popular uprising against Bavarian rule. Early skirmishes saw the Tyrolese gain temporary control of Innsbruck. More fighting resulted in 20,000 rebels taking control of the city. After defeating the Austrians at the battle of Wagram, Napoleon sent 40,000 French and Bavarian troops to retake Innsbruck. At the Battle of Bergisel (13–14 August), Hofer's Tyrolean partisans inflicted one of the few defeats suffered by Napoleon's troops. For two months Hofer led the city from the Hofburg, ruling as 'Commandant of the Tirol' in the name of the Austrian Emperor. A further defeat of the Austrian army led to isolation of the rebels, who fled to the mountains. After a final stand with diminishing forces, Hofer was defeated and forced into hiding. Captured in early 1810, he was taken to Italy, tried and on Napoleon's specific orders, executed by firing squad. In 1834, Hofer's body was returned to Innsbruck and interred in the Hofkirche in a small grave near Maximilian's massive (empty) tomb. A monument to Hofer was erected at Bergisel in front of a museum containing a panorama of his famous victory. The Tyrolean state anthem *Zu Mantua in Banden* tells the story of Hofer's tragic fate and execution.

Innsbruck's new ski-jump towers over Bergisel, with Nordkette behind

To visit **Bergisel** (635m), continue ahead past the tram terminus to the Bierstindl cultural inn, and ascend Klostergasse R, turning L onto Bergisel trail at the point where the alley leads into Brennerstrasse. At Bergisel, you will find the **Andreas Hofer monument** and Kaiserschutzen museum commemorating Tyrolean resistance against Napoleon in 1809. A little further on is the **Olympic ski jump**. Retrace your steps to the tram terminus (15mins round trip).

STAGE 13
Patscherkofel to Tulfeinalm

Start	Patscherkofelhaus (1964m)
Finish	Tulfeinalm (2035m)
Distance	7km
Ascent	200m
Descent	100m
Grade	red
Time	2hrs 30mins
Highest point	Rote Wand (2055m)
Maps	AV31/5 (1:50,000)
	FB241 (1:50,000)
	K36 (1:50,000)

The head of the eagle is a short walk along the Zirbenweg, overlooking Innsbruck from high on the slopes of Patscherkofel, south of the Inn Valley. A wonderful chance to look back at the mountains already visited and a chance to preview some of those to come. The start is reached by tram and cablecar with return to the city by chairlift, bus and train. *Zirbe* is German for pine, and the Zirbenweg traverses one of the best natural pine forests in the eastern Alps. Educational panels (in German) along the route provide information about the forest.

First you have to reach the start of the stage at Patscherkofel. Take a bus (route J from Hungerburg via city centre, every 15mins) or tram (route 6 from Bergisel tram terminus, hourly) to reach the pretty village of **Igls** (tourist office, all services, wide choice of hotels and guesthouses), which sits on a grassy terrace 300m above Innsbruck. The bus takes you all the way to the Patscherkofelbahn cablecar station, but the tram terminates just below the village. Walk on along the path beyond the terminus to reach the village centre. Turn L at the main street, and walk up to the cablecar (late May to early October 0900–1630, tel 0512 377234, two stages,

See map on pp134–135

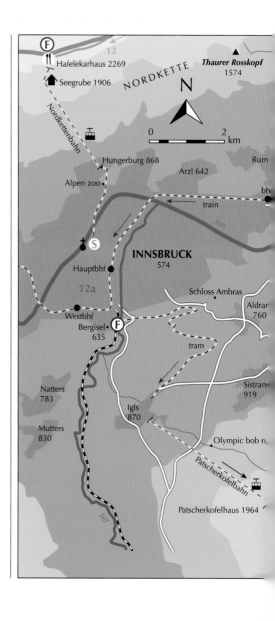

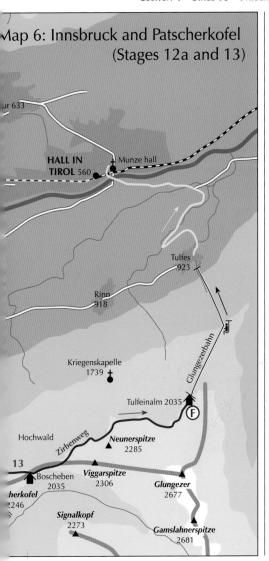

Map 6: Innsbruck and Patscherkofel
(Stages 12a and 13)

ur 633

HALL IN
TIROL 560   Munze hall

Tulfes
923

Rinn
918

Kriegenskapelle
1739

Glungezerbahn

Tulfeinalm 2035
Ⓕ

Hochwald   Zirbenweg   Neunerspitze
2285

13

Boscheben
2035   Viggarspitze
2306   Glungezer
2677

herkofel
2246

Signalkopf
2273   Gamslahnerspitze
2681

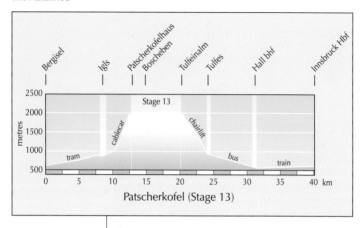

Patscherkofel (Stage 13)

Zirbenweg, with magnificent views over the Inn valley and snow-capped Zugspitze (right)

total journey time 20mins; round trip tickets are available, ascending by Patscherkofelbahn and descending by Glungezerbahn to Tulfes). On the way up, just before the middle station, the cablecar passes the Olympic bobsleigh run L.

At the top, start walking from outside the
Patscherkofelhaus (officially known as Schutzhaus)
(1964m) (OeAV, 31 beds 16b/15d, meals/refresh-
ments, late May to early October, tel 0512 377196)
where you bear half L heading NE (sp Tulfeinalm)
along **Zirbenweg**. For the whole walk, the view L is of
Innsbruck and Hall below, with the Karwendelgebirge
dominating the far side of the Inn valley. Looking down
the valley, all the mountains encountered so far can be
seen with Wilderkaiser in the distance, while up the
valley, you can see the mountains to come. The path
contours for 2.2km below Patscherkofel, bearing R at
a path junction, and passing just below **Boscheben**
refuge (2035m) (private, 19 beds, prior reservation
required as refuge is unmanned at night, meals until
1500/refreshments, late May to early October, tel 0650
3792541) (45mins).

Continue heading E (sp Tulfeinalm), first south of
the ridge with views down into Muhltal, then passing
through a notch back to the north. Ignore a turn L, to
reach a second path junction (15mins).

*Boscheben refuge, with
Patscherkofel visible on
the right*

Turn L to continue on Zirbenweg, bearing NE away from the ridge and pass below Viggarspitze (2306m). Winding around the flanks of the mountain with gentle undulations, the path eventually rounds a bend R (with perhaps the best view of the lower Inn valley) where the ski paraphernalia of Tulfeinalm comes into view. Rounding a coomb with a ski run below, you reach **Tulfeinalm** (2035m) (private, 12 beds 12b/0d, meals/refreshments, June to end of September, tel 05223 78153) (1hr 30mins).

From Tulfeinalm, the Adlerweg descends to the village of Tulfes using the two-stage **Glungezerbahn** chairlift which can be found slightly above and 300m beyond the refuge (early July to mid-September, 0830–1200, 1300–1630, journey time 40mins, tel 05223 78321). ◄

It is possible to walk down, using a well graded 4wd track that zigzags through the trees beneath the chairlift.

From **Tulfes** (923m) (tourist office, meals/refreshments, accommodation) there is a regular bus service (route 4134, hourly) to the ancient medieval city of **Hall in Tirol**, from where you can catch a train back to Innsbruck. Alternatively, you can catch the same bus route, in the opposite direction, directly to **Innsbruck**.

A DOUBLE OLYMPIC CITY

Innsbruck is one of only three cities (the others are St Moritz and Lake Placid) to have held the winter Olympic Games twice. The 1964 games were the first winter Olympics to attract over 1000 competitors. The second was in 1976, when Denver withdrew for financial reasons and Innsbruck was a late replacement. The downhill ski races were held on Patscherkofel with the other alpine events at Axamer Lizum. The bobsleigh and toboggan run is on the slopes above Igls, while the ice stadium for the indoor events is between the railway station and the autobahn. The Austrian ski legend Franz Klammer, won his only gold medal here in 1976 at the age of 22.

The most dominant element of winter sport architecture, the Bergiselschanze ski-jump hill overlooking the city, is a replacement for the original concrete Olympic hill on the same site. The new hill, opened in 2002, was designed by the Iraqi born, London based architect Zaha Hadid, who was also responsible for the new Hungerburg funicular. One notable feature of the Innsbruck ski-jump, which features on television every New Year as the site of the third round of the Four Hills Tournament, is that it over-looks Innsbruck's main cemetery. A particularly chilling reminder to every competitor, as they hurtle down the slope, of the need to be careful!

STAGE 14
Hochzirl to Solsteinhaus

Start	Hochzirl bahnhof (922m)
Finish	Solsteinhaus (1806m)
Distance	7km
Ascent	900m
Descent	–
Grade	red
Time	2hr45min
Highest point	Solsteinhaus (1806m)
Maps	AV5/1 (1:25,000)
	FB5322 (1:25,000); or 322 (1:50,000)
	K26 (1:50,000)

This short stage starts at Innsbruck Hauptbahnhof with a train journey on the Mittenwald line to Hochzirl. Then a steep ascent on 4wd tracks and paths to Solsteinhaus, which can be seen on the ridge above when emerging from the forest.

To reach the start of the stage, take a Mittenwaldbahn train (destination Scharnitz, Garmish or Munchen, hourly, journey time 23mins) from Innsbruck Hauptbahnhof, and alight at Hochzirl. The line climbs steadily away from Innsbruck with views over the valley. Hochzirl station is soon after the 2km Martinswand tunnel.

See map on pp140–141

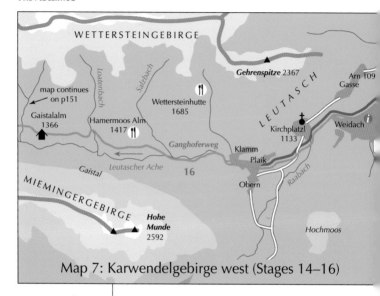

Map 7: Karwendelgebirge west (Stages 14–16)

At **Hochzirl** (922m), leave the station by the ramp at the E end of platform 2 (to the rear of the train) and follow a path parallel to the railway leading into the woods. Cross a small forest track and after 500m turn L at a 4wd track (sp Solsteinhaus) and start ascending very steeply NE (10mins).

Pass a house and continue ascending to reach another 4wd track. Turn R and continue up through the trees. This brings you out onto yet another wide track, which leads R around a sharp hairpin bend (40mins).

Ignore the first steep uphill track L immediately after the bend (which Kompass wrongly shows as Adlerweg), and take the second fork L 25m further on (sp Solsteinhaus). Follow this track contouring through the trees below Garbersalm. Pass a series of small goods lifts serving chalets at Garbersalm and come out onto a 4wd track at another hairpin bend. Turn L, following this track past Solsteinhaus goods lift R at Thomasegg Overbach and along the side of a deep gorge with sheer limestone

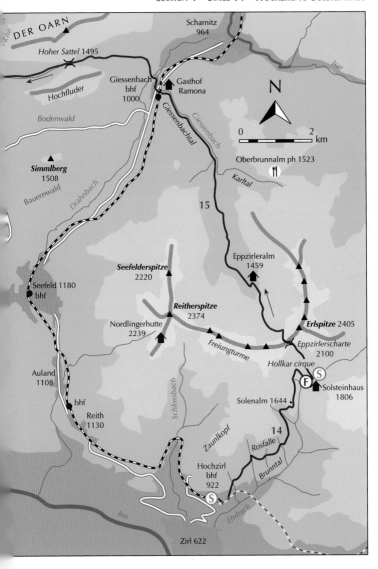

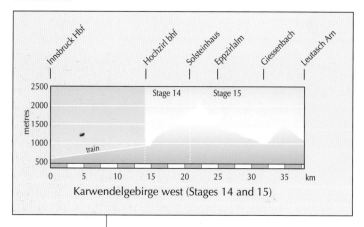

Innsbruck Hbf Hochzirl bhf Solsteinhaus Eppzirlalm Giessenbach Leutasch Arn

Stage 14   Stage 15

metres

2500
2000
1500
1000
500

train

0   5   10   15   20   25   30   35   km

Karwendelgebirge west (Stages 14 and 15)

cliffs R, to reach a barrier marking the end of vehicular access (40mins).

Looking up to Solsteinhaus on a bluff above the head of Brunntal

Drop down to cross the rocky washout of a river coming down from L, which is often dry by mid-summer. The precise crossing place varies depending on winter flood damage. Head for a yellow sign on a grassy bank

above the rocks on the other side, about 100m upstream. Turn R, bearing E, and zigzag up through the now thinning trees. At a clearing, by a stanchion for the goods lift, turn sharply L heading N through meadows past a chalet to **Solenalm** ski hut L (1644m) (30mins).

The view from Solsteinhaus over a cloud filled Inn valley to Stubaier Alpen

Both Solsteinhaus R and Erlspitze (2405m) are now in view above, with Eppzirlerscharte notch L and the route of the next stage crossing the scree to the notch clearly visible. Continuing through the trees, the path rises to cross a side valley. It then descends slightly to cross the washouts of two rivers below Hollkar cirque. From here it is a straightforward ascent on a good path SE through dwarf conifers to **Solsteinhaus** (1806m) (OeAV, 104 beds 49b/55d, mid-May to mid-October, tel 05232 81557) (45mins).

143

SECTION 5
WETTERSTEINGEBIRGE AND MIEMINGERGEBIRGE

STAGE 15
Solsteinhaus to Leutasch

Start	Solsteinhaus (1806m)
Finish	Leutasch Arn (1094m)
Distance	17km
Ascent	800m
Descent	1500m
Grade	red
Time	6hrs (plus 20mins walk into Leutasch)
Highest point	Eppzirlerscharte (2100m)
Maps	AV5/1 and 4/3 (1:25,000)
	FB5322 (1:25,000); or 322 (1:50,000)
	K26 (1:50,000)

This challenging farewell to the Karwendelgebirge requires a steep ascent up scree and rock to Eppzirlerscharte notch. Then a long descent through meadows and the Giessenbachklamm gorge to cross the railway and main road at Giessenbach. The final part brings a straightforward ascent and descent on forest tracks through the foothills of the Wettersteingebirge, ending in the sprawling resort of Leutasch.

See map on pp140–141

Leave from the rear of **Solsteinhaus** by the climbing wall, and head NW across grassy slopes dotted with dwarf conifers (sp Eppzirleralm). From above the refuge, the route of the Adlerweg up to Eppzirlerscharte notch is clearly seen. Ascending gently at first, the gradient steepens as the scree and rock beneath Erlspitze is reached. The path climbs around the head of **Hollkar cirque**, with a short cable-aided section, and starts to

zigzag up over scree. A path L leads to Nordlinger refuge via *klettersteig*. Continue zigzagging up over rock and scree first on R, then crossing L, to reach the ridge at **Eppzirlerscharte** notch. The exact point where you cross the ridge is not obvious until the very last moment. As you climb, there are a number of amazing rock formations and spires visible on the ridge to both sides (2100m) (1hr 10mins).

From beautifully modernised Solsteinhaus, the Adlerweg climbs across the screes to Eppzirlerscharte notch

The notch is a good place to pause and admire the view. Your next target, Eppzirleralm refuge, can be seen surrounded by meadows at the head of the valley far below. The zigzag descent over scree is every bit as steep as the ascent. Part way down, before the end of the zigzags, a path L contours below Freiungturme. Keep R, heading down into sparse grass and dwarf conifers. In the meadow at the bottom of the descent, cross the wide washout of a stream coming down from Erlspitze between a series of dams, and turn L onto a good track leading to **Eppzirleralm** refuge (1459m) (private, 17beds 6b/11d, mid-May to mid-October, tel 0664 6525307) (1hr).

The Adlerweg descends to Eppzirleralm gasthof, seen below, then along Giessenbachtal valley

From the refuge it is a simple matter of following the 4wd track as it descends steadily for 6km all the way down the valley to Giessenbach. The valley, broad with meadows at first, becomes steadily narrower and thickly forested as you descend. After 500m the track re-crosses the washout and after another 750m runs along an earth embankment marking the end of the washout. After passing a series of meadows below R, the track passes through a gate. At 4km from the refuge, the dirt road descends a moraine to join another 4wd track coming down a side valley R from Oberbrunnalm refuge. Continue ahead descending steadily along the main valley, now called **Giessenbachtal**, which deepens to become a narrow tree and cliff-lined gorge. The river is crossed eight times. A sharp bend L, crossing the river for the last time, brings the gorge to an end at a car park, where it emerges into the valley carrying the main road from Seefeld to Scharnitz and the railway from Innsbruck to Munich (1hr 30mins).

Continue ahead, crossing the railway and passing a factory L, to reach the main road in **Griessenbach**. Cross the road and continue ahead. Turn R (sp Scharnitz) at the next street, parallel with the main road. At the end of this street, R, is **Gasthof Ramona**, (1000m) (private, 35 beds, meals, tel 05213 5541, taxi service, trains to Munich and Innsbruck) (5mins).

From the car park beside the gasthof, take the last turn L, just before the river (sp Leutasch). Fork L to reach a stream. Bear R, crossing the stream and at a complicated path junction take the 4wd track ahead heading NNW (sp Leutasch uber Hoher Sattel). This track crosses an area used for dog sledges and ski/archery contests and ascends steeply with views of Scharnitz R. Sparse tree cover at first becomes thicker as the track bears L to head W into the Sattelklamm gorge.

After 1.5km, the 4wd track ends. Continue on a path ahead through the trees, which soon bears R, zigzagging to gain height above the valley floor. As you ascend the gorge, the limestone outcrops L become very impressive. The path continues climbing along the side of the valley for 400m until it reaches the start of a 4wd track leading to Leutasch. Another 400m of gentle ascent along this road brings you to a chalet R and the summit at **Hoher Sattel** (1495m) (1hr 30mins).

The good 4wd track descends steadily through the woods down the Satteltal valley, dropping 400m in 3km to reach a bridge over the Leutascher Ache River at **Arn** (1094m) (45mins).

This is the official end of Stage 15, but it makes sense to cross the bridge and continue a short distance following the footpath L alongside the river (sp Leutasch Weidach). Cross back over the river at the first bridge and continue following the river to the second bridge. Turn L to reach **Weidach**. This is the beginning of the very spread-out year-round resort of **Leutasch** (all services, wide choice of hotels and guesthouses, tourist office tel 0508 8010, bus to Seefeld) (20mins).

LUDWIG GANGHOFER'S HUNTING PARADISE

Although German by birth, the writer and novelist Ludwig Ganghofer set many of his novels in the area around Leutasch. Born in 1855 he originally trained to be an engineer before switching to study literature and philosophy. He spent some years in Vienna working as a playwright and journalist before coming to Tillfussalm in 1891, where he purchased Haus Hubertus, a hunting lodge. His Alpine homeland novels earned him the sobriquet of a 'world of good' writer. His works, which describe the life of simple, competent, honest people, are nowadays thought of as kitsch, not least because most of them are set within a background of idyllic Bavarian and Tyrolean scenery.

During WW1, he worked as a war correspondent, producing reports with strong patriotic and nationalist overtones, and published anthologies of war poems. A close friend and strong supporter of Kaiser Wilhelm II, his reports often lauded the way the war was conducted and just before Germany's final capitulation he was still writing stirring calls to carry on fighting. He died soon after the war in 1920.

Many of Ganghofer's works, particularly his novels, are still in print, and he is estimated to have sold over 30 million copies. He is one of the most 'filmed' of all German writers, 34 of his novels having been adapted for cinema or television, particularly during the Heimat film era after WW2. His best known novels include *Castle Hubertus*, *Forest Fever* and *The Edelweiss King*.

STAGE 16
Leutasch to Ehrwald

Start	Leutasch Arn (1094m)
Finish	Ehrwald (1000m)
Distance	25km
Ascent	600m
Descent	700m
Grade	white
Time	6hrs 30mins
Highest point	above Igelsee (1600m)
Maps	AV4/3 and 4/2 (1:25,000)
	FB5322 (1:25,000) and 352 (1:50,000); or 322 (1:50,000)
	K5 (1:50,000)

A long gentle ascent through meadows following the Leutascher Ache river to its source at Igelsee lake, followed by a steeper (but still easy) descent. The path connects two ski resorts, Leutasch which extends for 6km along the valley, and Ehrwald standing below the towering SW face of Germany's highest mountain Zugspitze (2962m). The trail coincides for part of its length with a very popular off-road cycle route.

The stage starts with an easy walk through the spread-out communities that make up **Leutasch**. Wherever you start, head for the Leutascher Ache River and join a good track following the river W. Leaving **Weidach**, this track can be found L of the river.

Stage 16 is shown as far as **Gaistalalm** on p140, and continues on pp150–151.

Follow the track upstream passing **Kirchplatzl** (1136m), the main commercial centre of Leutasch, on the opposite bank. Continue through Aue, Plazl and **Obern**, passing Plaik and finally **Klamm** on the other side of the river (55mins from Weidach).

Continue on L of river (sp Almenparadies Gaistal) ignoring an Adlerweg sign pointing across the bridge. At St Joseph, 900m after Klamm, ignore the path turning uphill and cross the river on an iron bridge. The path only stays on the R bank for 100m before crossing back to L on another bridge (15mins).

Follow the track upstream on the L of the river. On the opposite bank, there is a long series of car parks for day visitors to the valley ahead. After 1.5km cross the river for the last time, following the track L, R, and L again around a series of zigzags. Just before the last car park (which can be seen ahead through the trees), turn L and soon bear R (sp Gaistalalm, Tillfussalm) onto a 4wd track winding up into the woods. This is **Ganghoferweg** (30mins).

This path climbs about 100m above the river through the trees. Fork L and emerge from the woods into an area of meadows and scattered trees, passing below **Hamermoos Alm** refuge (private, no accommodation, meals/refreshments, tel 0676 333 7000) which can be seen across the meadows R. Cross the vehicular access

149

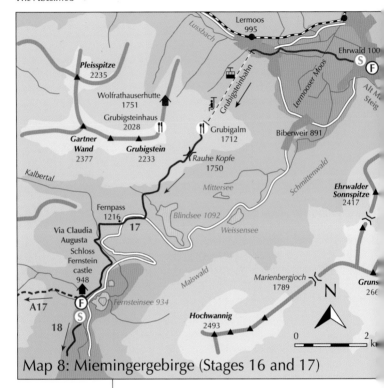

Map 8: Miemingergebirge (Stages 16 and 17)

track for the refuge. Bear R at next path junction (sp Gaistalalm) and ascend to cross a stream in a side valley. Continue through woods, emerging into a meadow where you will find **Gaistalalm** refuge (1366m) (private, 9 beds 0b/9d, meals/refreshments, mid-May to October, tel 05214 5190) (1hr).

Leave the refuge on a path (sp Tillfussalm) heading NW through meadows to the woods ahead. Cross a stream by a footbridge. Emerging from the woods, the path passes between **Haus Hubertus**, the hunting lodge and writing retreat of Ludwig Ganghofer, and **Tillfussalm** refuge (1382m) (private, no accommodation, meals/

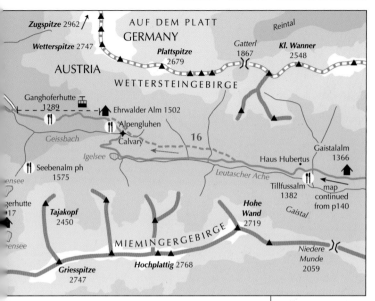

refreshments, end of May to October, tel 05214 6297) (15mins).

Pass the main entrance to the hunting lodge and follow the 4wd track downhill towards the river, to rejoin the dirt road through the valley. Turn R (sp Ehrwalder Alm) and continue ascending gently, alternating between woods and meadows. This is a popular mountain bike route and care needs to be taken. After 1.7km, reach a fork in the tracks (30mins). Both branches lead to Ehrwald. ▶

The R track is slightly shorter, but climbs higher and is the more popular with mountain bikers.

The L track is the official route of the Adlerweg. Forking L, follow the steadily narrowing river upstream passing below a chalet at Feldernalm. Continue through a gate and past a chairlift bottom station to emerge into a large bowl-shaped meadow. By late summer this is often dry, but in spring and in wet weather it contains a picturesque lake, **Igelsee** (55mins).

Zugspitze towers above Igelsee lake, which fills with water after heavy rain

The track passes N of Igelsee, ascending through trees to reach a hairpin bend, with a track L to Seebenalm, a popular day walk destination from Ehrwald. Keep R, soon reaching the summit of the track (1600m), where a view of Ehrwald opens up below L, with the S face of Zugspitze

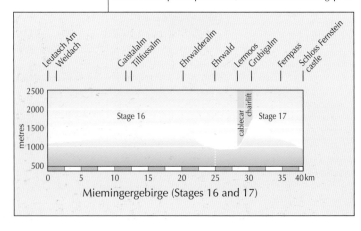

Miemingergebirge (Stages 16 and 17)

(2962m) towering above. Head downhill around a series of hairpins, passing a Calvary scene R carved into the rock face of one bend, to reach **Alpengluhen** Gasthof (private, no accommodation, meals/refreshments, tel 05673 2349) and **Ehrwalder Alm** refuge (1502m) (private, 39 beds, meals/refreshments, late May to mid-October, tel 05673 2534) (40mins).

At Ehrwalder Alm there is a cablecar which could be used to shorten the descent to Ehrwald. However, the Adlerweg does not officially use this cablecar, preferring the easy walk down through meadows and grassy ski runs.

Take the 4wd track W (sp Ehrwald nach Weisenweg) descending the ski run L of the cablecar. This winds in and out of the trees, passing **Ganghoferhutte** (1289m) (private, no accommodation, meals/refreshments, late June to mid-October, Friday/Saturday/Sunday only, tel 0664 1431357). The track continues down to reach

Ehrwald parish church with Zugspitze behind

a path junction just above the cablecar bottom station (1108m) (40mins).

Take a path passing L of the cablecar station (sp Altmuhlenweg), dropping down to the corner of the car park. Turn L into trees and cross the stream by a bridge. Turn R on **Alt Muhl Steig**, following the stream downhill. At the end of the path cross back over the stream. Fork R at a road junction then bear R to cross a meadow and emerge between houses at the top of **Ehrwald** village green. Turn L and follow the road down to the village centre. The tourist office is on R just before the church (1000m) (all services, wide choice of hotels and guesthouses, tourist office tel 05673 20000 208) (30mins).

GERMANY'S HIGHEST MOUNTAIN

Part of the Wettersteingebirge, Zugspitze (2962m) is the highest mountain in Germany, but only the 53rd highest in Austria. The border between the two countries goes over the summit, where there used to be a customs post, but since Schengen (see Introduction), this is no longer staffed. The name derives from the German *lawinenzug* (avalanche route) of which there are many on the mountain's steep northern slopes. The first recorded ascent was in 1820 by three German surveyors led by Lt Josef Naus. However, DAV have discovered a map dated 1770, showing that local people had climbed the mountain at least 50 years earlier.

The summit can be reached by climbing or walking (allow two days), by mountain railway from Garmish (ascending inside the mountain) or by two different cablecar routes. One goes up from Eibsee in Germany, the other from near Ehrwald (mid-May to end of October 0840–1640, 20mins journey time). As a result, the summit is often crowded with day trippers. There is a mountain refuge at the top, Munchnerhaus (DAV, 30 beds 0b/30d, meals/refreshments, mid-May to early October, tel 0049 8821 2901), also restaurants and bars associated with the railway and cablecars. The views are outstanding, with Munich 90km away visible on a clear day.

For a short period after WW2, the US military took over the old summit hotel for exclusive use of military and civilian employees. Full board was $1 a day with ski lessons extra at 25 cents an hour. It is rather more expensive today!

STAGE 17

Ehrwald to Schloss Fernstein castle

Start	Ehrwald (1000m)
Finish	Schloss Fernstein castle (948m)
Distance	11km
Ascent	–
Descent	800m
Grade	white (Lermooser Moos), red (Fern Pass)
Time	3hrs 15mins (plus 20mins cablecar/chairlift ascent)
Highest point	Rauhe Kopfe (1750m)
Maps	AV4/1 (1:25,000)
	FB352 (1:50,000)
	K5 (1:50,000)

In reality, two short walks with a cablecar and chairlift ride in between to whisk walkers up to Grubigalm. The first walk crosses the flat Lermooser Moos, a dried up lake bed. The second winds down the Fern Pass through forests with idyllic views of Blindsee and Fernsteinsee lakes. Part of the trail follows the route of the Via Claudia Augusta, the ancient Roman road from Verona to Augsburg.

Leave **Ehrwald** on Moosweg. This starts between the Spar supermarket and Hotel Grunen Baum, on the main road in the centre of the village, and drops down SW to cross the dried up lake bed of **Lermooser Moos** on a surfaced track. Turn R (sp Lermoos) at the first path junction, and head W on a surfaced track between fields. Lermoos is visible ahead, with Grubigstein rising behind. Bear L and R, continuing W to reach a golf course. Cross the main canalised drainage channel and continue ahead with the golf course R. A sign indicates where the Adlerweg crosses the Claudia Augusta roman road. Continue through more fields to arrive on a main road at the edge of **Lermoos** (995m).

See map on p150

It's an easy walk from Ehrwald to Lermoos across the pastures of Lermooser Moos

Turn L and follow this road round two bends to reach Unterdorf, the commercial centre of Lermoos (995m) (all services, wide range of accommodation, trains to Garmish and Reutte, tourist office tel 05673 20000300), and the base station of **Grubigsteinbahn cablecar** L (end of May to mid-October 0900–1630, journey time 20mins, tel 05673 2323) (55mins).

At the top of the cablecar continue by chairlift to **Grubigalm** (1720m) (private, no accommodation, meals/refreshments, open when cablecar operating, 0930–1730, tel 05673 4262). Follow a track passing under the third stage of the chairlift and fork L (sp Fernpass) on a path winding through trees with occasional clearings. This ascends gently to soon reach the summit at **Rauhe Kopfe** (1750m), and then descends, gently at first but steepening as the trees give way to dwarf conifers. Looking down through the trees, you catch glimpses of turquoise Blindsee lake far below. High on the mountainside ahead you can see Loreahutte on Stage A17. The path zigzags down into a coomb and up the other side, before turning L at a path junction and continuing down to join the main road over **Fernpass** (1216m) (1hr 15mins).

Turn R and follow the level road for 700m to the old Fernpass Hotel (closed) and café. **Great care is needed here as this is a major road without footpaths!** (10mins).

Fork R in front of the hotel, leaving the main road, and continue on the surfaced road descending into **Kalbertal** valley. After passing a barrier and chapel R, this becomes a 4wd track. At the washout of the river, turn L and follow the riverbank on the shingle beach. Ignore a fork R (sp mountain bike route to Schloss Fernstein) and continue L towards a bend on the main road visible above and ahead. Just before this bend, fork R (sp Schloss Fernstein) to follow a path down through the woods between road and river. Cross the footbridge over the river and fork R uphill (30mins).

You are now on the route of **Via Claudia Augusta**, an ancient Roman road from Verona to Augsburg. This runs downhill as a 4wd track, parallel to the main road, passing under an archway through **Schloss Fernstein castle**.

Schloss Fernstein castle

To reach the main road and hotel (of which the castle is nowadays an annexe), turn L after the castle, and follow a track round to the hotel entrance (948m) (private, accommodation, meals/refreshments, open all year, buses to Nassereith and Reutte, tel 05265 5210) (25mins).

WHERE ROMAN ARMIES CROSSED THE ALPS

In 15BC, General Nero Claudius Drusus, the adopted son of Roman emperor Augustus, decided to improve communications between the south and north of the Alps to support military manoeuvres in Noricum and Rhaetia (present day Austria and Bavaria). The project of converting a pack animal trail into a track capable of taking wheeled vehicles over the Alps took 60 years to accomplish, being completed by Emperor Claudius in AD47. The completed road was named Via Claudia Augusta, and ran north from Ostiglia in the Italian Po valley, to reach Augsburg, the principal Roman town of southern Germany. En route it crossed the main alpine barrier over the Reschenpass, and continued over the Fernpass, between the Wettersteingebirge and Lechtal Alps. The Adlerweg follows this route for a short distance on the south side of Fernpass.

A road intended initially for military purposes soon became the main Roman trading artery between the Mediterranean and central Europe, with regular posting stations where provisions were available and fresh horses stabled. Some of these, like Bolzano, grew into sizable Roman towns that are still important today. It was joined, in the second century AD, by a road over the Brenner Pass. The route still exists, indeed a number of long abandoned stages have been rediscovered, and the Via Claudia Augusta is now a popular walking and cycling route in Austria and Germany.

SECTION 6
LECHTAL AND VALLUGA

STAGE 18
Schloss Fernstein castle to Anhalterhutte

Start	Schloss Fernstein castle (948m)
Finish	Anhalterhutte (2042m)
Distance	16km
Ascent	1350m
Descent	250m
Grade	red
Time	5hrs 45mins
Highest point	Hinterbergjoch col (2202m)
Maps	AV4/1 and 3/4 (1:25,000)
	FB352 (1:50,000)
	K24 (1:50,000)

The route follows a 4wd road through forest up the remote Tegestal valley to reach high pastoral meadows around Hintere Tarrentonalm pasture hut. Continuing to climb, the path eventually emerges onto Hinterbergjoch. Here a very steep, short descent and ascent across scree leads over Kromsattel to Anhalterhutte.

Leave **Schloss Fernstein castle** by the Via Claudia Augusta Roman road, following it SW from behind the hotel. Cross the river by a bridge, descending S. Pass a path R, where the high-level alternative Stage A17 turns off for Loreahutte, and join the surfaced road that links the hotel with the campsite. Continue past the campsite. Turn R 100m after the end of campsite (sp Tarrentonalm) onto a 4wd track leading into the woods. Follow this gently undulating track, forking R (sp Nassereith) at a path junction. The track

See map on pp160–161

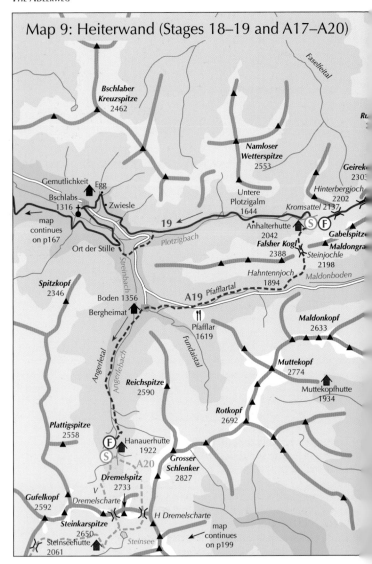

Map 9: Heiterwand (Stages 18–19 and A17–A20)

Bschlaber
Kreuzspitze
2462

Namloser
Wetterspitze
2553

Faselfeital

Geireke
2303

Gemütlichkeit   Egg
Bschlabs
1316

Untere
Plotzigalm
1644

Hinterbergjoch
2202

Kromsattel 2137

Zwiesle

map
continues
on p167

19

Anhalterhütte
2042

Gabelspitz

Falsher Kogl
2388

Maldongra

Ort der Stille

Plotzigbach

Steinjochle
2198

Steinbach

Hahntennjoch
1894

Maldonboden

Spitzkopf
2346

Boden 1356

Pfafflartal

A19

Maldonkopf
2633

Bergheimat

Pfafflar
1619

Angerlebach

Fundaistal

Muttekopf
2774

Muttekopfhütte
1934

Angerletal

Reichspitze
2590

Rotkopf
2692

Plattigspitze
2558

Hanauerhütte
1922

A20

Grosser
Schlenker
2827

Gufelkopf
2592

Dremelspitz
2733

V
Dremelscharte

H Dremelscharte

Steinkarspitze
2650

Steinseehütte
2061

Steinsee

map
continues
on p199

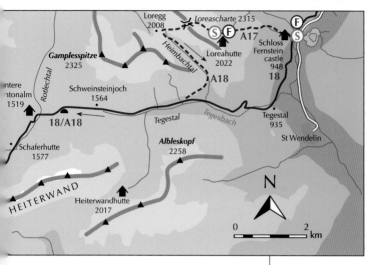

closely follows the route of an electricity supply line before emerging into **Tegestal** valley (935m) (30mins).

Turn R (sp Tarrentonalm), to head W on a good 4wd track running the full length of the valley. A series of steep hairpins and a short tunnel takes the track 200m up a moraine. Continue to ascend, less steeply, along a well-forested deep valley. The alternative route via Loreahutte, Stage A18, joins R immediately after a bridge over a small stream (1hr).

Continue along the 4wd track, bearing R uphill at a track fork. The tree cover thins out and occasional meadows appear. Pass a ruined farm L to reach a col just beyond **Schweinsteinjoch** beside a seasonal lake (1564m). Continue ahead, descending slightly and bear R at a track fork. Pass an abandoned zinc mine L. Turn L at a path junction to reach **Hintere Tarrentonalm** farm and alpine pasture hut (1519m) (private, 5 beds 0b/5d, basic meals/refreshments, mid-June to mid-September, tel 05412 61131) (1hr).

Leave Tarrentonalm via a gate through the farmyard and head SW on a 4wd track turning sharply R after

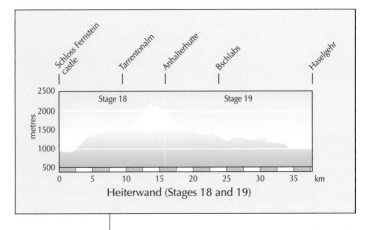

Heiterwand (Stages 18 and 19)

200m. At the next junction turn L (sp Anhalterhutte) following a 4wd track that leads to a chalet at **Schaferhutte** R (15mins).

Looking up Rotlechtal, with the Heiterwand cliffs flanking the valley

The 4wd track ends here, and a faint path continues ahead ascending the valley. Trees give way to dwarf pines, and these in turn give way to grassy slopes with

rocky outcrops and scree tongues. Waymarking is by paint flashes on rocks and free standing metal posts. After 1.5km, the valley bears slightly R (45mins).

At this point, the path zigzags steeply up a moraine, and then continues to gain height climbing steadily along the R side of the valley above. The formidable wall and spires of Heiterwand L dominate the view across the valley, while looking back Zugspitze can be seen clearly. The sheer face of Heiterwand is an excellent sounding board and the noise of sheep bleating on the hillsides high above is often reflected with a surreal echoing tone. The path ascends across a grassy hillside with occasional rocky outcrops and scree tongues. A final path up the side of the scree brings the path to the col at **Hinterbergjoch** (2202m) (1hr 15mins).

This is a very impressive spot. A deep bowl ahead marks the cirque at the head of Faselfeiltal valley, which drops away R, while Gabelspitze (2581m) towers above L. The next target for the Adlerweg, Kromsattel col, can be seen straight ahead on the other side of the bowl. The path crosses the wooden fence on the col by a stile and drops very steeply into the cirque ahead, so take care in

Anhalterhutte with Maldongrat rising behind

selecting the correct line of descent. Do not be tempted by what looks like a route straight down. Instead, turn R (sp Anhalterhutte) along the rim past some large boulders to a sign painted on rocks. Here a path zigzags into the bottom of the bowl then cuts across the scree to **Kromsattel** (2137m) (40mins).

From the col a path leads steadily down WSW across grassy slopes to **Anhalterhutte**, which can soon be seen ahead (2042m) (DAV, 89 beds 14b/75d, meals/refreshments, mid-June to end of September, tel 0664 461 8993) (20mins).

STAGE 19
Anhalterhutte to Haselgehr

Start	Anhalterhutte (2038m)
Finish	Haselgehr (1006m)
Distance	22km
Ascent	250m
Descent	1250m
Grade	red
Time	6hrs
Highest point	Anhalterhutte (2038m)
Maps	AV3/4 and 2/2 (1:25,000)
	FB352 or 351 (1:50,000)
	K24 (1:50,000)

A long descent, first over open mountainsides and then through the ever deepening Plotzigtal valley. After Bschlabs the route drops into Holltal to reach the 'Place of Silence'. There is a short ascent through forest, before a 4wd track is followed above Bschlabertal and down into Lechtal.

Leave **Anhalterhutte** on the lower of two paths (sp Bschlabs), contouring around the head of Plotzigtal immediately N from the refuge. After 400m fork L and

From Anhalterhutte the Adlerweg descends across Plotzigalm and down the valley towards Bschlabertal

continue descending, bearing round to head W. The path descends over grassy slopes with occasional rocky outcrops, aiming for the corner of the forest in the valley below. The final part of this descent is on a heavily eroded path parallel to a rocky streambed. Cross this streambed and pass below the bottom corner of the forest (30mins).

Continue descending with the main riverbed L, until just past the barns on the opposite side of the river at **Untere Plotzigalm** (1644m). Here the way ahead has been blocked by a series of washouts. Paint marks on rocks indicate a way down and across the river. Once over the river turn R on a path and continue parallel to the river to join a track descending from Plotzigalm. After 500m this drops down to the river, where paint marks on rocks show the way back to the R bank.

The path climbs above the river to reach a stile, then contours through the forest, gradually gaining height relative to the river. A main road with a hairpin bend comes into view through the trees below (1425m) (1hr 10mins).

Stage 19 is shown as far as **Bschlabs** on p160, and continues on p167.

A path L offers an alternative route cutting out the circuitous route ahead through Bschlabs. Follow the path down into the valley (sp Bschlabs via Holltal), cross first Beferwaldbach and then Streinbach streams by footbridges and rejoin the Adlerweg on the opposite side of Holltal, saving 3km.

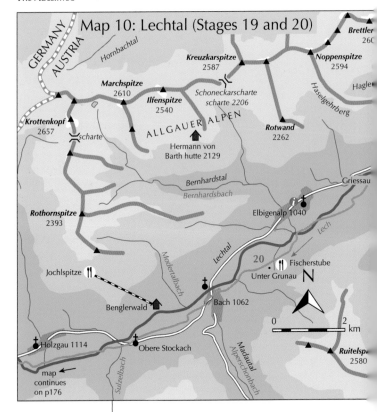

Map 10: Lechtal (Stages 19 and 20)

Soon afterwards, the side valley that you have been following emerges into the much larger Holltal valley. At this point, the path crosses a 4wd track at a hairpin bend. Follow the uphill track R (sp Bschlabs Hohenweg) for 50m then branch off L. The path bears R to follow Holltal NW. Looking L up Holltal, Dremelspitz can be seen above the head of the valley, with Hanauerhutte perched on a ledge. A detour is made around a coomb L. Soon afterwards, a second much larger detour is made above the little village

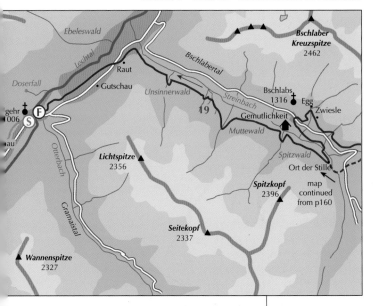

of Bschlabs. The path first climbs to pass on a short surfaced section through the hamlet of **Zwiesle**, then crosses a meadow. After a path junction R, it drops down L to cross a stream and climbs up the other side with the hamlet of **Egg** visible on the ridge above. The path finally turns S downhill, picking up a road. This leads through a series of hairpin bends and passes a number of vernacular wooden log buildings, to emerge beside Gasthof **Gemutlichkeit** in the centre of **Bschlabs** (1316m) (private, 40 beds, open all year, meals/refreshments, tel 05635 259) (50mins).

Cross the main road and leave the village by a track immediately R of the church (sp Lechtal). Bear L behind the church and follow this path, the Weg der Sinne, as it descends through woods to the river. Cross the wooden suspension bridge over Streinbach brook and climb steeply on the opposite bank to reach the **Ort der Stille** (place of silence) (30mins).

AN ACOUSTIC DEAD ZONE: 'THE PLACE OF SILENCE'

The little village of Bschlabs sits perched on the edge of a gorge. Below is the Weg der Sinne (path of senses), leading to the Ort der Stille (place of silence). This is an outdoor sculpture park spread along a winding footpath leading to the river at the bottom of the gorge. A poem – *Morning Walk* – starts the path, followed by a large wood-carved figure, 'The Listener'. 'The Wanderer Shows the Way', carved from the rock beside a bridge, is followed by another wooden sculpture – 'Three Silhouettes, Feel See Hear Nature'. Next comes a large wood-carving of a couple holding a newborn baby – 'The Child a Gift from God', by a woodcarver from Elbigenalp. Another poem – *I Drink the Good Air* – and a wood-carving of a wife supporting the body of her soldier husband with a spear through his body – 'A Returning to the Homeland' – are found before the river is reached.

Across the river, a poem – *Praise the Water* (adapted from a canticle of St Francis) – is followed by a mosaic of plastic pieces set into the cliffside called 'Inspiration and Contemplation' and a 'Prayer of the Elderly People' by St Teresa of Avila. The path now arrives at the 'Place of Silence' – a seat set in a bend of the gorge between two cliffs that deaden the sound of the river. This is claimed to be acoustic zero, 'absolute silence in the chasm of a torrent'. The artworks end with two more pieces, a painting of traditional Tyrolean costume from Pfafflar and a wind harp hanging in the trees.

Continue ascending to reach a 4wd track. Turn R, and follow this track along the S side of Bschlabertal valley. A series of hairpins, passing a feeding station for deer, takes the track down into and across a deep sided valley. The track continues contouring for 1.5km until it ends suddenly, overlooking Unsinnertal (1hr 5mins).

It is 1km on faint forest paths to the start of another 4wd track. There are paint markings on trees, but some have disappeared where there has been forest clearance. Continue SW for 200m along Unsinnertal to cross the river by a wooden bridge. Turn back N and head up into the woods to reach the ridgeline. Drop down a little to cross two large clearings where trees have been cut down to give clear sight lines for hunting platforms. Continue along the crest of a small ridge before dropping down L to cross a stream and pick up the next 4wd track (25mins).

'The Listener', one of the woodcarvings on Weg der Sinne

Follow this for 3.5km, contouring along the S side of **Bschlabertal** and passing round a number of coombs. The track eventually descends to reach the main road through **Lechtal** (45mins).

The official Adlerweg turns R to follow a path circling a wooded peninsula between the Streinbach and Lech rivers. This uninteresting diversion can be avoided by turning L on a side road parallel to the main road. At a timber yard in **Raut**, drop down R and cross the road by an underpass. Turn L onto a surfaced path heading SW through fields with occasional barns, to regain the Adlerweg. This brings you to the banks of the River Lech 500m downstream from Haselgehr. Continue along the riverbank to reach **Haselgehr bridge**. The stage ends just over the bridge at **Haselgehr church** (1006m) (choice of hotels and guesthouses, meals/refreshments, shops, bus service) (45mins).

STAGE 20

Haselgehr to Steeg

Start	Haselgehr (1006m)
Finish	Steeg (1124m)
Distance	20km
Ascent	120m
Descent	–
Grade	white
Time	4hrs 30mins
Highest point	Steeg (1124m)
Maps	AV2/2 and 3/3 (1:25,000)
	FB351 (1:50,000)
	K24 (1:50,000)

An almost level walk along the pastoral Lechtal valley, passing villages famous for the use of a distinctive form of wall painting known as *Luftimalerei* that adorns many houses. The route is mostly along surfaced paths through fields, sometimes along the banks of the Lech. A frequent bus service operates along the main road through the valley from Haselgehr to Steeg.

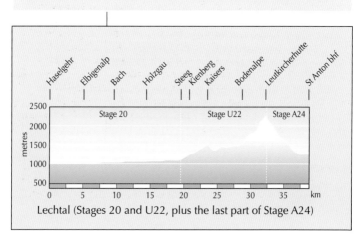

Lechtal (Stages 20 and U22, plus the last part of Stage A24)

Following severe floods that swept away many bridges, several new footbridges have been built over the Lech

The stage starts at **Haselgehr church**. Follow the main road for 150m and fork R before a barn onto a surfaced track. Cross a junction (sp Griessau) and continue above the houses parallel with the main road. You are now heading SW, and will head in this direction for 20km. Continue out of Haselgehr through fields and a farmyard at **Schonau**. At Ort, turn R along the main road for 100m and then L (sp Elbigenalp) to reach the river. Turn R alongside the river to **Griessau** bridge (45mins).

Turn L over the bridge into Griessau, bear R and cross a stream. Continue out of the village for 1km on a path between fields, curving L to reach a minor road. Turn R and, with the trees on your L, follow this road to reach the river. After 1km, cross the river on a new bridge (one of a number of impressive new bridges built since a devastating flood a few years ago) and turn immediately L along the opposite bank (30mins). ▶

Stage 20 is shown as far as **Holzgau** on p166, and continues on p176.

To visit **Elbigenalp** continue ahead after crossing the bridge (tourist office tel 05634 5315, accommodation, meals/refreshments, all services, bus service, woodcarving school and museum) (10mins).

There are a variety of routes between Elbigenalp and Steeg following both banks of the river, and you may be faced with junctions where Steeg is signposted in both directions! Do not worry; so long as you head upstream you will reach Steeg whichever path you choose.

Follow the river, crossing back to the south bank at the next new bridge (sp Grunau and Bach). Turn R to follow the river on a path winding through trees. After a little while, this path moves away from the river and continues with trees L and fields R, through the little hamlet of **Unter Grunau** and the **Fischerstube** (meals/refreshments, 1100–2300, closed Tuesday). Walk on through Obergrunau, bearing L to reach the river again and continue to **Bach** (accommodation, meals/refreshments, supermarket, bus service) (50mins).

Cross the bridge over Alperschonbach and turn L to follow the main road through the village. Just after a supermarket R, fork R on a path through fields. After 500m, turn L (sp Steeg cycle path) and after another 100m turn R. Continue for 1.5km, passing frequent barns and a small wayside chapel L, with Unter Stockach away L. When this path ends, turn L to reach the church at **Obere Stockach** (35mins).

Turn R and follow the main road through the village. Where the road bears R to cross the river, do not cross

Luftmalerei (air painting) is a common form of decoration in Lechtal, particularly in Holzgau

172

but continue ahead across a side stream (sp Holzgau) with the river R to reach after 500m a footbridge R. Cross the river and turn L, along the north bank with Holzgau visible ahead, to reach a bridge over a side stream after 1.5km (40mins).

The path passes S of **Holzgau** (1114m) (tourist office, accommodation, meals/refreshments, all services). To reach the village, famous for its Luftlmalerei house decoration, turn R before the bridge and follow a path into the village (10mins). Kompass shows the Adlerweg between Stockach and Steeg using Jochweg, a rough path along the opposite (south) side of the river.

Continue along the riverside (sp Steeg) before turning away at a fork R. Soon after turn L and cross to the south bank at the next bridge. Turn R, continuing to follow the river past a bridge and through **Durnau** (20mins).

The path moves a little away from the river past the Hammerle apartment complex L. 500m after Durnau, cross the river on another new bridge. Turn L along the N

LUFTLMALEREI: WHIMSICAL DECORATION IN LECHTAL

Many houses in the Lechtal valley are decorated in a style known as *Luftlmalerei*, literally 'air painting'. This style, which originated in Southern Bavaria, is a rustic combination of *trompe l'oeil* and late baroque. The name comes from a house called Zum Luftl in Oberammergau where Franz Zwink (1748–1792) pioneered the style. Images often have a religious theme, but not necessarily so, and are usually whimsical in character. Most are painted on the facade, where the colour lasts for about three generations, but others are found inside.

The trompe l'oeil element is usually found in painting an appearance of architectural features, such as architraves, ledges and window surrounds, which in reality do not exist. The baroque is provided by whimsical characters somehow overlaid on the facade, such as people balanced on a ledge or floating on a cloud. Some of the best examples in Lechtal can be found in Holzgau. These include Dengeleshaus (Dorfplatz 49), Doppelhaus (Heimat museum 34/35), Adeg-Markt Hammerle (50), and Lippa-Franzhaus (32).

A carved golden eagle statue in Steeg

bank to follow the river for 800m and then continue on a path through fields. At an offset path junction, turn R and immediately L, passing S of **Hagerau** (1107m) (accommodation, meals/refreshments, supermarket, bus service) (25mins).

At a T-junction turn L. Upon reaching the river turn L, walking a short distance downstream, to cross the river and then turn R on a path through fields lined with barns to **Dickenau**. Pass a road L leading to Kaisers, which is the route of the alternative Stage U22 to Leutkircherhutte, and reach the end of the stage at **Steeg** bridge (1124m) (tourist office, accommodation, meals/refreshments, all services, bus service) (25mins).

Between Steeg and St Anton, the Adlerweg crosses the spine of Lechtaler Alpen. The main route (Stages 21–23) goes via Krabachtal and crosses the ridge at Pazielfernerscharte, close to the summit of Valluga. This route can be challenging, particularly in poor weather. An easier alternative (Stage U22) goes via Almajurtal to Leutkircherhutte, then descends to St Anton following Stage A24.

STAGE 21
Steeg to Stuttgarterhutte

Start	Steeg (1124m)
Finish	Stuttgarterhutte (2305m)
Distance	14km
Ascent	1200m
Descent	50m
Grade	red
Time	5hrs
Highest point	Stuttgarterhutte (2305m)
Maps	AV3/2 (1:25,000)
	FB351 (1:50,000)
	K24 (1:50,000)

A steady climb on a 4wd track through forest to a high pastoral valley with a number of seasonal farms. The path eventually emerges onto Krabachjoch saddle, the westernmost point of the Adlerweg on the border between Tyrol and Voralberg. From here, there are breathtaking views of green peaks and the Pazuelferner glacier to the south.

Start N of the bridge in the centre of **Steeg**, and follow the main road W. After 300m cross over the river on the next bridge by Steeg church. Turn R (sp Prenten) and follow a surfaced road for 700m to **Welzau** farm. The road becomes a farm track and continues across a field. Turn L at a T-junction and R to follow the track around a field. Continue ahead as the track leads back to a surfaced road by the river. Follow the river past a small bridge to rejoin the main road S of Prenten bridge. Walk along the side of the road for 100m and turn L (sp Stuttgarterhutte) onto a grassy path zigzagging up into the trees (30mins).

See map on pp176–177

Turn R onto a path ascending above the little village of **Prenten**. Follow this path through the trees, bearing L at a crossroads, Rotes Kreuz, to emerge onto a good 4wd track where you turn L. You are now at the mouth of

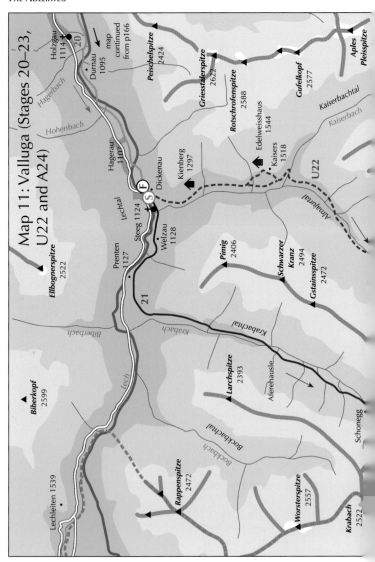

Map 11: Valluga (Stages 20–23, U22 and A24)

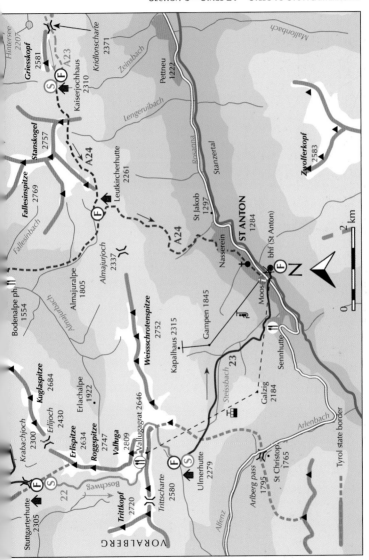

Hintersee 2207
Griesskopf 2581
A23
Kridlonscharte 2371
Mallonbach
Kaiserjochhaus 2310
Zeinsbach
Pettneu 1222
Lengeruibach
Stanskogel 2757
A24
Leutkircherhutte 2261
Rosanna
Stanzertal
Fallesinspitze 2769
Zwolferkopf 2583
Fallesinbach
St Jakob 1297
ST ANTON 1284
bhf (St Anton)
Almajuralpe 1805
Almajurjoch 2337
A24
Nasserein
N
Bodenalpe ph 1554
Almalnbach
Gampen 1845
Moos
2 km
Weissschrotenspitze 2752
Kapalhaus 2315
Kuglaspitze 2684
Erljoch 2430
Erlachalpe 1922
Steissbach
Galzig 2184
Sennhutte
Erlispitze 2634
Roggspitze 2747
Valluga 2809
Krabachjoch 2300
Vallugagrat 2646
23
Arlenbach
Boschweg
Trittscharte 2580
Ulmerhutte 2279
St Christoph 1765
Tyrol state border
Stuttgarterhutte 2305
22
Trittkopf 2720
Arlberg pass 1795
Alfenz
VORALBERG

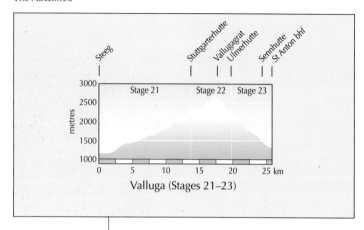

Valluga (Stages 21–23)

Krabachtal, and the track continues for 7km, ascending steadily to serve seasonal farms far up the valley (30mins).

The 4wd track first keeps to the L of the valley, contouring along the valley side through trees, high above the river. It crosses a number of side streams where washouts caused by winter melt waters occasionally breach the track. There are good views into the gorge below. At one point, a path leads down to a crossing of the river, where a ladder allows access to a hut high on the other side of the valley. As the track ascends, patches of snow that may remain all year are seen in the valley below. When the stream below melts the lower levels, the upper snow is sometimes left forming fantastic ice bridges over the stream. Halfway along the valley, the track descends to a bridge over the stream (1hr).

Zigzag up the other side of the gorge. From here to the end of the valley, the track stays R of the river. The valley broadens slightly and the track emerges above the trees into high alpine pasture with grazing cattle in summer. The track fords a number of streams that are often dry by summer. However, after heavy rain these streams may need to be waded across. A number of small seasonal farms and barns are passed, at the last of which, **Schonegg** (1740m) the 4wd track ends (1hr).

Waterfalls at the head of Krabachtal in spate after heavy rain

TAKING THE COWS UP THE MOUNTAIN, AND BRINGING THEM DOWN AGAIN

One feature of alpine dairy farming is the large amount of high altitude pastureland. As you walk through in summer it seems only natural to hear cowbells and see cattle grazing on top of a mountain pass, but behind the scenes a lot of activity goes into making this possible. Transhumance farming involves taking the herds up the mountain every spring. In days gone by, the cowman would often stay in the mountains, sleeping in shepherds' huts for the summer. Nowadays most farmers make the daily commute by 4wd car, shepherd's buggy or trials bike, returning home each day after checking on their cattle. Some valleys, like Krabachtal, still have a number of inhabited high altitude farms and huts that are used in summer only.

Every autumn, farming villages throughout the Tyrol celebrate *Almabetriebsfest* – when the cows are brought back down the mountain to their winter quarters. The cows are usually dressed for the occasion with garlands of wild flowers wrapped round their horns, and then paraded through the village. Much beer is consumed (by the farmers, not the cows!) as part of the celebration. In the past farmers would take this opportunity to count their neighbours' cows and assess how rich (or poor) they were. The cows then spend a few weeks grazing valley pastures, before being put into barns for the winter.

Continue through pastures on a rough track which eventually becomes a path. This is an area very popular with marmots, which can be heard and seen on both sides of the path. After 1.2km, detour R, then turn back L to ascend a moraine and reach an upper pasture with **Furmesgumpalpe** cowman's hut (2015m) set back from the path L. Cross the pasture to a boggy washout from a stream coming down from Krabachspitze R (1hr).

Cross this washout and follow the path across grassy slopes as it bears R below the screes of Fanggekarspitze L. As you ascend, Stuttgarterhutte comes into view on the ridge ahead. A long steady ascent W over more grassy slopes, with a sharp turn L, brings you to the ridge at **Krabachjoch** saddle (2300m). Bear L and continue ascending for a short distance along the ridge to reach **Stuttgarterhutte** (2310m) (DAV, 66 beds 21b/45d, meals/refreshments, mid-June to late September, tel 05583 3412) (1hr).

STAGE 22
Stuttgarterhutte to Ulmerhutte

Start	Stuttgarterhutte (2305m)
Finish	Ulmerhutte (2279m)
Distance	6km
Ascent	400m
Descent	450m
Grade	black
Time	3hrs 15mins
Highest point	Pazielfernerscharte (2713m)
Maps	AV3/2 (1:25,000)
	FB351 (1:50,000)
	K24 (1:50,000)

This stage originally involved a crossing of Pazielferner glacier and a scramble through Trittscharte notch. Unfortunately, persistent rockfalls have rendered this route too dangerous and a replacement route now goes via Valluga. This is still a challenging route however, and should not be undertaken lightly, particularly in inclement weather. After a straightforward start, the path climbs steeply up scree and rocks to the col below the summit of Valluga. A steep scramble down from the col to Vallugagrat cablecar station is followed by a descent over snowfields to Ulmerhutte.

Almost all of this stage is in Voralberg, where waymarks follow a different scheme to Tyrol. Signposts are white, not yellow, with wanderweg indicated by yellow flashes, roter bergweg with red and schwarzer bergweg with blue. This stage is blue.

Leave **Stuttgarterhutte** on Boschweg, heading S (sp Valluga) and contouring below the W face of Erlispitze. Tussock grass soon gives way to steep rocky slopes with tongues of scree. There are excellent views ahead of

See map on pp176–177

Pazielferner glacier and Trittkopf. The path is cut into the cliff face with cables for security, and later descends into and out of a coomb. Continue below Roggspitze and Valluga, to reach a path junction where the original route via Trittscharte notch turns R (1hr 5mins).

A path, with some scrambling and exposed sections, continues up the ridge L to reach the cablecar station on the summit of Valluga (2809m) (15mins).

Bear L (sp Valluga) to reach an area of large scree and boulders. Scramble up this steep rocky slope, keeping to the R, taking care to follow waymarks painted on occasional rocks. At the top bear L to reach the ridge, where a glimpse can be obtained of Ulmerhutte directly below, and continue up past avalanche protection barriers R to Pazielfernerscharte col overlooking Jahnturm (2713m) (50mins). ◄

The main path (sp Ulmerhutte) drops down steeply ahead from the col into the bowl beneath the S face of Valluga. Keep R on the rocky slope close to the cliffs and scramble down to the middle station of the Valluga cablecar at **Vallugagrat** (2646m) (meals/refreshments, open to late September, 0825–1620) (25mins).

Vallugagrat seen from Jahnturm, with the cablecar ascending to Valluga's summit

Descend E, eventually bearing S, on a path keeping to R of wide bowl below Valluga. Snow often remains in the bottom of the bowl all year. Continue bearing R to reach a path junction at Valfagehrjoch col (2543m) (30mins).

Turn R and follow the path SW down through a desolate barren man-made landscape of ski tows, chair-lifts and reservoirs for snow making equipment. Head towards the communications tower that can be seen ahead, aiming to pass R of it. **Ulmerhutte** is a short distance past this tower (2279m) (DAV, 50 beds 18b/32d), mid-July to mid-September, tel 05446 30200) (25mins).

Ulmerhutte beneath the face of Pazielfernerspitze, with Trittscharte notch and Trittkopf to the left

STAGE 23
Ulmerhutte to St Anton am Arlberg

Start	Ulmerhutte (2279m)
Finish	St Anton am Arlberg (1284m)
Distance	6km
Ascent	–
Descent	1000m
Grade	red
Time	2hrs
Highest point	Ulmerhutte (2279m)
Maps	AV3/2 (1:25,000)
	FB351 (1:50,000)
	K24 (1:50,000)

The final stage of the Adlerweg is a pleasant stroll, winding steadily downhill through the ski runs, chairlifts and cablecars that serve the slopes above St Anton.

See map on p177

Leave **Ulmerhutte** on a good 4wd track heading SE through wide alpine pastures, and follow this downhill forking L after 250m. Continue until you pass above a reservoir R. Fork L (sp St Anton), onto a path leading down Steissbachtal valley. This path leads into another 4wd road meandering along the deep chasm of Steissbachtal. Continue ahead to reach a fork (1hr).

Fork R, and immediately take a small path R parallel to and slightly above the track. The track crosses and re-crosses the river. This short path enables you to avoid these two fords and keep your feet dry. After 100m rejoin the track and continue descending with the river L. Pass the lower station of Zammermoosbahn chairlift L, soon getting a first view of St Anton, and continue until Galzigbahn cablecar passes overhead (20mins).

The final descent of the Adlerweg through Steissbachtal

Turn L, and zigzag down a path on the R side of the ski run. Pass a depot for piste equipment R and join a 4wd track past **Sennhutte** R (1500m) (no accommodation, meals/refreshments). Follow the track around a hairpin R. Pass a flood protection dam L and turn sharp L at a road junction. Turn almost immediately R onto Muhltobelweg (sp St Anton) an attractive path that goes down through a gorge with walkways above the river. This emerges by a small park where a notice board and a large eagle mosaic herald the end of the Adlerweg. Congratulations!

Continue downhill for a few more metres to the centre of **St Anton** (1301m) where welcome refreshments can be found (all services, wide choice of accommodation, restaurants, tourist office tel 05446 22690, trains to Bregenz, Innsbruck and beyond) (40mins).

ST ANTON AM ARLBERG, CRADLE OF ALPINE SKIING

For many centuries, St Anton was a quiet backwater in a remote corner of Tyrol. There was a narrow mule track over the Arlberg pass along which some trading, mostly of salt, occurred. In 1824, the track was widened and surfaced, enabling wheeled transport to use it. Soon after, in the 1840s, the British surveyed the route as a possible rail link to Egypt, but this came to nothing. It was not until 1884 that the 10km Arlberg rail tunnel was opened, putting St Anton on a key east/west route through the Alps (Arlberg is the watershed between rivers flowing to the North Sea and to the Black Sea). The town became a stopping point for the 'Arlberg Orient Express', which provided a first-class only *wagons lits* service from Paris to Budapest, with a connection from London.

The coming of the railway opened St Anton and the Arlberg region to tourists. Originally coming mostly for the delights of summer, the formation of the Ski Club in 1901 and the pioneering efforts of some of Europe's first ski instructors led to St Anton developing into a world-class winter sports resort. Today the Arlberg ski region, of which St Anton is the largest part, is the third most important skiing area in Tyrol, with a long season from late November to late April/early May. There is 262km piste and 184km off-piste skiing, served by 82 lifts, 10 of which are cablecars. It held the world skiing championships in 2001. The town has a wide variety of accommodation and many restaurants and bars making it an ideal place to relax and celebrate the conclusion of your Adlerweg walk.

Kandaharhaus museum in St Anton is right beside the end of the Adlerweg

To find out more about the history of St Anton and its role as the cradle of alpine skiing, you should visit Kandaharhaus, the local history museum housed in a wooden chalet that was once a hotel, built in 1912 (10 Rudi Matt Weg, beside the end of the Adlerweg, mid-June to end of September, open afternoons from 1200, closed Monday, restaurant).

For details of onward transport from St Anton, see 'Getting there' in the Introduction.

STAGE U22
Steeg to Leutkircherhutte

Start	Steeg (1124m)
Finish	Leutkircherhutte (2261m)
Distance	13km
Ascent	1300m
Descent	150m
Grade	red
Time	5hrs (5hrs 30mins via Kaisers)
Highest point	Leutkircherhutte (2261m)
Maps	AV3/2 (1:25,000)
	FB351 (1:50,000)
	K24 (1:50,000)

This variant enables you to bypass the steep rocky scramble over the shoulder of Valluga by using Almajurtal to cross the Lechtaler Alpen ridge instead of Krabachtal. It follows a surfaced road ascending from Steeg to Kaisers, then continues along a 4wd track and a path ascending through forest and alpine meadows to Leutkircherhutte. To continue to St Anton, descend as described in Stage A24.

Leave **Steeg** by the main bridge, turning L along the S side of the river. Turn R at a sharp bend and head steeply uphill on a surfaced road (sp Kaisers). Continue around a series of hairpin bends and a short road tunnel. The gradient eases as the road contours along the side of Almajurtal valley, high above the river, to reach the tiny village of **Kienberg** (1297m) and Gasthof Alpenhof (accommodation, tel 05633 5616) (40mins).

See map on pp176–177

The road continues towards Kaisers, passing through avalanche shelters and after 700m reaches a fork (20mins). The direct route to Leutkircherhutte takes the lower fork R, contouring above the river and passing 150m below Kaisers.

The spread-out village of Kaisers

The upper fork L continues climbing, and after 1.5km reaches **Kaisers**, a community of isolated farms and guesthouses connected by the road as it zigzags up the hillside. Soon after the first farm R, there is a faint unsignposted field path L. This cuts off the zigzags and heads directly to **Edelweisshaus** at the top of the village (1544m) (DAV, 83 beds 27b/56d, meals/refreshments, May to end of October, tel 05633 5602). (If you miss the path, stay on the road around two hairpin bends to reach the *haus*). (45mins).

From the haus follow the surfaced road back downhill, past the church R and round a hairpin bend. Take a faint field path L, descending through meadows to rejoin the direct route to Leutkircherhutte in the valley below, where you turn L (15mins).

The direct track continues past chalets at Boden, and after being rejoined by the route through Kaisers, turns R to cross the river by a bridge. Bear R uphill on a surfaced road, which becomes a 4wd track after a junction (sp Leutkircherhutte). This track, which you follow for 4.5km, climbs gently SW along the side of Almajurtal valley. After 2km, drop down R to cross the river, crossing back after

a further 2km. At the point where the 4wd track forks just before **Bodenalpe** pasture hut, leave the track and turn L (sp Leutkircherhutte) across a meadow to pick up a path that enters the forest just R of the stream (1554m) (private, no accommodation, meals/refreshments, early June to mid-September) (1hr).

Weissschrofenspitze and Fallersteinspitze above the head of Almajurtal, from Almajurjoch col

Zigzag steeply up through the trees, bearing R at the top and continue alongside a meadow at Moos. Just before the path crosses the stream to reach Almajuralpe farm (1805m), turn L up through the trees (1hr 10mins).

Continue ascending, on an eroded path through shrubs and dwarf conifers, onto a grassy hillside with rocky outcrops above, to reach **Leutkircherhutte** which sits on the ridge L of Almajurjoch col (2261m) (DAV, 58beds 8b/50d, meals/refreshments, late June to late September, tel 0664 985 7849) (1hr 20mins). ▶

The remaining 6.5km (2hrs) of the route down into St Anton are described as part of Stage A24.

SECTION 7
LECHTALER ALPEN HOHENWEG

The Hohenweg consists of two separate sections, Stages A17/A18, which represent a variant between Schloss Fernstein castle and Tegestal taking in the very remote Loreahutte, and Stages A19 to A24, which offer a challenging high-level traverse of Lechtaler Alpen. The two sections are connected by Stage 18.

Four high-level stages (A20, A21, A22, A23) are classified as black. None of these stages is long, but with steep drops, narrow ledges aided by fixed chains and mostly above 2000m, they can be challenging, particularly in bad weather. The most difficult section is the Theodor Haas weg traverse of the SE face of Vorderseespitze (Stage A23), however this traverse can be avoided by taking an alternative route slightly lower down. However the Hohenweg requires no specialist equipment and should be achievable for most Adlerweg walkers.

STAGE A17
Schloss Fernstein castle to Loreahutte

Start	Schloss Fernstein castle (948m)
Finish	Loreahutte (2022m)
Distance	4km
Ascent	1150m
Descent	50m
Grade	red
Time	2hrs 30mins
Highest point	Loreahutte (2022m)
Maps	AV4/1 (1:25,000)
	FB352 (1:50,000)
	K24 (1:50,000)

This is the first, short stage of the Lechtaler Alpen Hohenweg. A steep ascent through the woods above Schloss Fernstein castle takes the Adlerweg up to the Loreahutte, situated in high alpine pastures with extensive views across the valleys below.

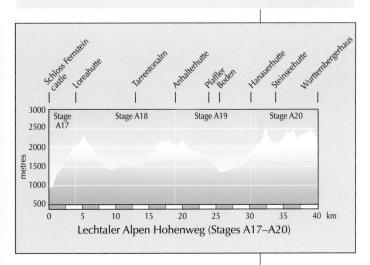

Lechtaler Alpen Hohenweg (Stages A17–A20)

Leave **Schloss Fernstein castle** by the Via Claudia Augusta Roman road, following it SW from behind the hotel. Cross the river by a bridge, descending S, then 50m before the point where Via Claudia Augusta and the surfaced road linking the hotel entrance with the campsite join, take a path R into the woods (sp Loreahutte). This ascends steeply with views through the trees back over the castle and Fernsteinsee lake. Pass Brandhutte L, continuing to zigzag up to reach a small clearing at Hirme Stalboden (1hr).

As you continue ascending, the trees thin and are replaced by dwarf conifers. At 1700m, pass a memorial to old comrades L, erected by AV members of Isartal section who operate the Loreahutte. The path soon emerges into high pastures. A path R leads to Loreaalm barns,

See map on pp160–161

191

The small self-service Loreahutte on the Hohenweg, with Loreascharte notch visible over its roof

while the main path bears L zigzagging over a final ridge to reach **Loreahutte** (2022m) (35 beds 0b/35d, self-service kitchen, usually manned at weekends July/August, at other times standard AV key opens door to kitchen, common room and dormitory) (1hr 30mins).

STAGE A18
Loreahutte to Anhalterhutte

Start	Loreahutte (2022m)
Finish	Anhalterhutte (2042m)
Distance	16km
Ascent	1200m
Descent	1200m
Grade	red
Time	3hrs (plus 4hrs 15mins described in Stage 18)
Highest point	Loreascharte notch (2315m)
Maps	AV4/1 and 3/4 (1:25,000)
	FB352 (1:50,000)
	K24 (1:50,000)

From Loreahutte, the path meanders across gently rolling high alpine pasture, before ascending to Loreascharte notch. It then drops into Heimbachtal valley to reach Tegestal valley. From here, follow Stage 18 as it climbs over Hinterbergjoch saddle to reach Anhalterhutte.

Leave **Loreahutte** by a gate behind the refuge and bear L heading W across high pastures (sp Anhalterhutte). The path, indistinct in places, is well waymarked by paint flashes on rocks. Bear R, heading NW with rocky scree

See map on
pp160–161

*Loreahutte in the
early morning with
Hochwannig across the
Fernpass*

rising L. At a path junction turn L and zigzag up a scree slope with rocky outcrops to reach **Loreascharte** notch (2315m) (50mins).

Descend W on an eroded path over grassy slopes with rocky outcrops, dropping into the bottom of **Heimbachtal** valley (2008m) (40mins).

Turn L and begin descending on R of stream. After a short distance cross the stream and continue on L. A faint path with occasional waymarks descends steadily, dropping over two rocky steps in the valley. Cross the stream to R for short distance and then re-cross to L. The path eventually crosses the stream for the last time, to turn SW towards Tegestal valley. This crossing point is not signposted. Look out for a little-used but obvious path rising above the opposite R bank, and cross the stream to reach this path. (If you continued along Heimbachtal you would soon start rising, heading away from the stream.) (1hr).

Head SW on a little-used and poorly waymarked path through the forest, rising a little at first before dropping to join the 4wd track running up **Tegestal**. Turn R (sp Tarentonalm) and follow the track to Hintere Tarrentonalm and **Anhalterhutte** as described in Stage 18 (30mins).

STAGE A19
Anhalterhutte to Hanauerhutte

Start	Anhalterhutte (2042m)
Finish	Hanauerhutte (1922m)
Distance	12km
Ascent	700m
Descent	800m
Grade	red
Time	4hrs 15mins
Highest point	Steinjochle col (2198m)
Maps	AV3/4 (1:25,000)
	FB351 (1:50,000)
	K24 (1:50,000)

The route climbs steeply S over Steinjochle col and descends to meet the road from Lechtal at Hahntennjoch. It follows this road W down Hahntennontal valley through the remote communities of Pfafflar and Boden, before turning S again to ascend Angerletal to Hanauerhutte, high above the head of the valley.

Leave **Anhalterhutte** SW (sp Hahntennjoch), dropping down a little to cross meadows with seasonal Kromsee lake L. Pass two small huts R and bear L, climbing round the corner of Maldongrat and continue ascending steeply across the hillside, above the screes of Falscher Kogl. A series of zigzags bring the path up the cliffs, with fixed cables for security, to reach **Steinjochle** col (2198m) (30mins).

See map on pp160–161

Descend across tussock grass, initially SE but soon bearing S, with the road pass between Boden and Imst visible below. Continue SW through dwarf conifers, dropping down to a point just before extensive car parking alongside the road at **Hahntennjoch** (1894m) (30mins).

Turn R (sp Boden) passing through a fence, and continue on a path through meadows parallel to the road descending towards Pfafflar. This path comes out beside a stream L, which is followed for 2km before joining the road at a sharp hairpin bend. Walk along the side of the road for 600m to the tiny community of Pfafflar (1619m) (Gasthaus **Pfafflar**, private, no accommodation, meals/refreshments, open 1000 to 1800, May to end of October, tel 0664 439 8560) (45mins).

Continue along the road for 250m and turn L over the stream onto a path that descends through trees and across meadows. Cross a 4wd track and after re-crossing the stream, join a second 4wd track for a short distance. Turn L off this track and follow a path down through meadows to the village of **Boden** (1356m) (Gasthof **Bergheimat**, private, 45 beds, meals/refreshments, tel 05635 231) (30mins).

Vernacular wooden housing in Boden

Cross the bridge just before the village and turn R (sp Angerletal) on a 4wd track. Fork R and drop downhill to cross the Angerlebach river. Turn L along a good track steadily ascending **Angerletal** for 3km. Looking ahead, Hanauerhutte comes into view perched above the end of the valley, with Dremelspitz (2733m) towering above. Shortly before the head of the valley, re-cross the river and arrive at the bottom station of Hanauerhutte goods lift L (1529m) (1hr).

From here, the path ascends the steepening valley through dwarf conifers and scrub, bridging two streams. Just after the second bridge, fork L and pass below the refuge. Turn R and zigzag up to reach the ridge 150m W of the refuge. Turn L to reach **Hanauerhutte** (1922m) (DAV, 138beds 38b/100d, meals/refreshments, mid-June to late September, tel 0664 2669149) (1 hr).

STAGE A20

Hanauerhutte to Wurttembergerhaus

Start	Hanauerhutte (1922m)
Finish	Wurttembergerhaus (2220m)
Distance	10km
Ascent	1200m
Descent	900m
Grade	black
Time	6hrs 15mins
Highest point	V Dremelscharte (2434m) or H Dremelscharte (2470m)
Maps	AV3/4 and 3/3 (1:25,000)
	FB351 (1:50,000)
	K24 (1:50,000)

A stage spent almost entirely above 2000m, during which four high-level cols are traversed. From Hanauerhutte a steady ascent across scree slopes to Vorderes Dremelscharte notch takes the Hohenweg over the main ridgeline of the Lechtaler Alps. A steep descent to tiny Steinsee lake is followed by a series of long contouring traverses on scree or tussock grass along the south side of the main ridge, rising and falling to cross three radial ridges en route. One of these crossings, Rosskarscharte, is the second most challenging part of Hohenweg.

Leave **Hanauerhutte** on a path S and after 75m reach a fork. Fork L (sp Steinseehutte). The other fork is a direct route to Wurttembergerhaus bypassing Dremelscharte. In 100m you reach another fork, with a choice of routes to Steinseehutte.

Stage 20 is shown as far as **Steinseehutte** on p160, and continues on p199.

Fork R for Vorderes Dremelscharte, passing a small lake L. The path starts ascending over tussock grass and through dwarf conifers. The going becomes rockier as the path gains height, with talus and scree replacing grass after 2100m altitude is reached. Continue zigzagging up a long scree and boulder filled gully between Dremelspitz (2733m) L and Schneekarlespitz (2641m)

Dremelspitz can
be crossed through
notches either
east (Hinteres
Dremelscharte)
or west (Vorderes
Dremelscharte) of the
summit. The eastern
route L is 1hr longer.

R to reach **Vorderes Dremelscharte** notch (2434m) (1hr 40mins). ◄

From the notch you can see **Steinsee** lake. Descend steeply SE down a gully with fixed cables for assistance. At the bottom of the gully, pass a path L leading down to Steinsee lake and bear R continuing to zigzag down. At the foot of the slope, join the path that has come from Hanauerhutte via the eastern notch. Turn R and descend gently over tussock grass to **Steinseehutte** (2061m) (OeAV, 84beds 24b/60d, meals/refreshments, mid-June to late September, tel 0664 275 3770) (50mins).

From the refuge, the path drops down a little N (sp Wurttembergerhaus) across grassy slopes through dwarf conifers to cross a stream, then rises steeply to a path junction below the shoulder of Schneekarlespitz.

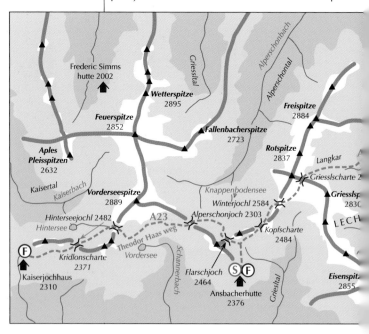

Turn L and contour below the screes of Steinkarspitz, heading for the gap ahead between Mittelkopf and Hintere Gufelkopf. Continue ahead ascending a grassy tongue with rocky outcrops, to reach a col (2302m) (1hr).

At the col turn R and ascend slightly to contour around the scree slopes of Gufelgras bowl, which can be seen ahead. Continue ahead at a path junction, passing just below Gufelgrasjoch col R. The bowl closes in ahead and the path continues contouring across the screes of Gufelspitz, up the R side of a wide gully. Near the head of the gully, painted signs indicate where the path

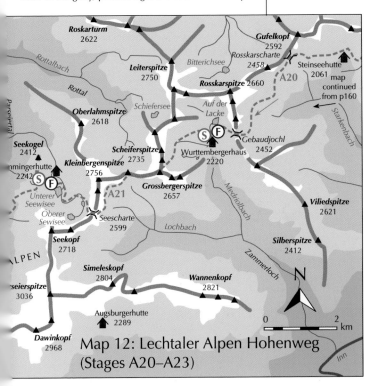

Map 12: Lechtaler Alpen Hohenweg (Stages A20–A23)

map continued from p160

turns uphill R, scrambling steeply over rocks to reach **Rosskarscharte** col (2458m) (45mins).

Over the col, the path drops steeply down 200m, first through a gully with fixed chains for assistance, then descends across scree, bearing L to reach sparse grass with rocky outcrops. Pass round the shoulder of Rosskopfe and bear R, ascending a little to contour across a mixture of rocky slopes and scree below Bitterichkopf. Pass the shoulder of Gebaudspitz R, and bear R to a path junction. Continue ahead and zigzag steeply up to **Gebaudjochl** col (2452m) (1hr 30mins).

From the col, you look across the Medriolbach valley with a track coming up from Zams in the Inn valley. Wurttembergerhaus is visible ahead perched on a bluff overlooking the valley. To get there however is not as straightforward as it looks. Turn L at the col, then bear back R across the scree slopes of Gebaudspitz to reach a path junction overlooking **Auf der Lacke** lake. Turn L, zigzag down the hillside and cross a small bridge to reach **Wurttembergerhaus** (2220m) (DAV, 63 beds 8b/55d, meals, end of June to mid-September, tel 0664 440 1244) (30mins).

Wurttembergerhaus is reached by a small bridge over a ravine

STAGE A21
Wurttembergerhaus to Memmingerhutte

Start	Wurttembergerhaus (2220m)
Finish	Memmingerhutte (2242m)
Distance	7km
Ascent	750m
Descent	750m
Grade	black
Time	5hrs
Highest point	Grossbergerspitze (2657m)
Maps	AV3/3 (1:25,000)
	FB351 (1:50,000)
	K24 (1:50,000)

A challenging high altitude stage, requiring mountain trekking experience and a good head for heights. Ascending over tussock grass, scree and bare rock, with sections aided by fixed cables, the path climbs onto the Lechtaler Alpen ridge. Following the ridge over a series of crests, including Grossbergspitze, the path provides awesome views in all directions. A final steep climb to Seescharte notch and a descent to Memmingerhutte.

From **Wurttembergerhaus**, take a path heading WNW (sp Memmingerhutte) contouring across the slopes of Ober Medriol. Rounding a coomb the path starts a long steady ascent SW towards the gap between Speissrutenspitz and Schieferspitz, which can be seen ahead. Initially across grassy slopes, the going becomes rockier after crossing a cleft.

See map on p199

Continue ascending across the screes below Sudturm and bear R, zigzagging up rocky slopes with Schieferscharte notch R. There is one short section with fixed cables for security. Turn R and circle a small inclined plateau anticlockwise to reach the summit ridge.

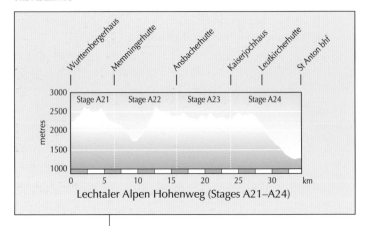

Lechtaler Alpen Hohenweg (Stages A21–A24)

Scramble along this ridge to reach **Grossbergerspitze** (2657m) (1hr 50mins).

From the summit, there are extensive views in all directions, with the east face of Parseierspitze dominating

Parseierspitze, on the left, is the highest point in North Kalkalpen (seen here from Grossbergspitze)

the view SW. Continue scrambling along the ridgeline, with some fixed cables, dropping down a little before rising to Grossbergkopf (2612m). Still following the ridge along an exposed crest, drop down to cross the head of Grossbergscharte notch (2493m). Shortly after the notch, drop down L, and contour across the rocky slopes and screes of Kleinberg. Down to the L is the deep Zammerloch valley and the path bears L contouring around the bowl high above the valley head. Bear R beneath Seeschartenspitze R, join a path coming up from Zams and ascend steeply to reach **Seescharte** notch (2599m) (1hr 55mins).

Memmingerhutte stands above Unterer Seewisee lake

Crossing the ridge the view down is a glaciated landscape of cirques and lakes sitting above the side of Parseiertal, with Memmingerhutte beyond. The path zigzags off the ridge, before bearing R to descend across rocky slopes. Cross the stream just below the outlet from Mittlerer Seewisee lake to reach a path junction (2409m) (30mins).

Turn R and follow the path down through a tiny ravine, then circle **Unterer Seewisee** lake L, to arrive at

Memmingerhutte (2242m) (DAV, 131 beds 21b/110d, meals/refreshments, mid-June to late September, tel 05634 6208) (45mins).

STAGE A22

Memmingerhutte to Ansbacherhutte

Start	Memmingerhutte (2242m)
Finish	Ansbacherhutte (2376m)
Distance	10km
Ascent	925m
Descent	775m
Grade	black
Time	6hrs
Highest point	Griesslscharte (2632m)
Maps	AV3/3 (1:25,000)
	FB351 (1:50,000)
	K24 (1:50,000)

Another challenging stage. A steep descent into Parseiertal valley is followed by an ascent up the screes of Langkar cirque (where snow may remain all year) and through a narrow chimney with fixed cables to Griesslscharte notch. The path then follows the main Lechtaler Alpen ridge, running just below the ridgeline, which is crossed two more times, before a short descent S to Ansbacherhutte and a first distant view of St Anton.

See map on pp198–199

Leave **Memmingerhutte** on a path N to reach a path junction after 150m. Turn L (sp Ansbacherhutte) and start descending diagonally across the hillside SW. For the next 3km the path drops down into **Parseiertal**, initially on grassy slopes but passing through patches of forest below 1900m altitude. As the path descends it crosses a number of side valleys. Just before the valley floor is reached a small metal bridge takes the path across a fissure in the hillside. At the bottom (1723m), cross the streambed by stepping stones, although the stream is often dry by mid-summer (1hr 20mins).

Turn R on the other bank, climbing diagonally away from the stream. Bear L round a shoulder of Griesslspitze and start the long ascent of **Langkar**. In the next 3.5km the path climbs continuously, gaining 900m in altitude. Initially contouring across grassy slopes to L of the valley, the path soon crosses the stream and zigzags up Schafgufel to reach a path junction (1977m) (50mins).

Bear L and continue ascending grassy slopes, now to the R of the valley. After 2100m altitude, the grass ends, the path continuing steeply up rocks and scree. From here to the col, patches of snow may remain all year. Towards the head of Langkar the gradient steepens and the path crosses to L of valley where fixed cables aid the final ascent up a narrow chimney to **Griesslscharte** notch (2632m) (2hrs).

The notch represents a crossing of the Lechtaler Alpen watershed, and between here and Ansbacherhutte the path remains close to the ridgeline, crossing it two more times. Circle a small boulder-filled cirque clockwise, then bear R descending gently across stony slopes where snow often lies all year. Views ahead are extensive with the Silvretta range, on the borders of Austria and Switzerland, visible on the horizon. The path drops down across the scree and rock of Oberes Griessl, then rises slightly to pass a path junction L and re-cross the ridge at **Winterjochl** (2528m) (40mins).

The path drops down a little on the north side of the col, then continues contouring across scree parallel to the ridge. The final crossing of the watershed involves a short steep scramble up **Kopfscharte** notch (2484m) (40mins).

Continue ascending gently for a short distance on grassy slopes along the S side of the ridge, then descend SW across scree, bearing R below Stierkopfl to reach a path junction. The path R leads to Kaiserjochhaus, and is the route of the next stage. Turn L, and contour across the

Griesslscharte notch and Rotspitze, with its red rock clearly visible

grassy slopes of Schafnock. Pass a path junction L, and ascend slightly to reach **Ansbacherhutte** (2376m) (DAV, 85 beds 27b/58d, meals/refreshments, early July to late September, tel 0664 143 1009) (30mins).

STAGE A23
Ansbacherhutte to Kaiserjochhaus

Start	Ansbacherhutte (2376m)
Finish	Kaiserjochhaus (2310m)
Distance	8km
Ascent	500m
Descent	600m
Grade	black
Time	4hrs
Highest point	Hinterseejochl (2482m)
Maps	AV3/3 (1:25,000)
	FB351 (1:50,000)
	K24 (1:50,000)

Another challenging high-level route with stiff ascents, vertical drop-offs, scree and rock. The path rises and falls over two cols before following the Theodor Haas weg across the SE face of rugged Vorderseespitze with steep drop-offs protected by fixed cables. Two more cols are crossed, as the path wanders from side to side across the Lechtaler Alpen ridge, before descending across scree to Kaiserjochhaus.

This stage starts by contouring N from **Ansbacherhutte** over grassy slopes, returning up the Schafnock ridge, which was descended at the end of Stage A22. After 600m fork L (sp Kaiserjochhaus), ascending gently across the scree below Stierkopfl, to cross the ridge at **Flarschjoch** (2464m) (25mins).

Over the col, the path drops 50m zigzagging down to cross a small karst lake, then continues descending gently across the scree to a path junction. Fork L, continuing to descend across scree to a grassy col with a shelter and a series of path junctions at **Alperschonjoch** (2303m) (30mins).

The route from here to Hinterseejochl uses the **Theodor Haas weg**, a path across the rocky SE face of

See map on p198

Crossing Vorderseespitze by the Theodor Haas weg, one of the trickiest sections of the Hohenweg (photo: Thomas Thiel)

To avoid this, drop down from Alpersonjoch to about 1900m altitude and turn R to follow a path ascending past Vordersee lake L. Rejoin the main path about 250m beyond the lake.

Vorderseespitze. ◄ Continue ahead W, descending a little over grassy slopes before rising to contour across the exposed face of the mountain, with steep drop-offs and fixed cables for security. Contour across the scree of Verborgene Pleis cirque, staying about 50m above **Vordersee** lake, then bear R zigzagging steeply up to **Hinterseejochl** (2482m) (1hr 35mins).

Cross the col and zigzag down the other side towards the bowl of Kridlon cirque. Turn L at a path junction and continue descending before contouring across the screes below Furglerspitze, Aperiesspitze and Kridlonspitze with Hintersee lake below R. The path ascends, aided by fixed cables and rungs to **Kridlonscharte** notch (2371m), between Kridlonspitze and Kreuzkopf, where there is a view down into Stanzertal far below (40mins).

Drop down from the notch SW across grassy slopes and a boulder field, then scramble up a rocky hillside below Kreuzkopf and Griesskopf, aided by fixed cables, carefully following the red paint flashes as it is easy to go wrong. Zigzag up a grassy ridge and descend a little to reach **Kaiserjochhaus**, which can be seen on the col below (2310m) (DAV, 67 beds 12b/55d, meals, mid-June to mid-September, tel 05672 71084) (50mins).

STAGE A24

Kaiserjochhaus to St Anton am Arlberg

Start	Kaiserjochhaus (2310m)
Finish	St Anton (1284m)
Distance	11km
Ascent	250m
Descent	1250m
Grade	red
Time	4hrs
Highest point	Schindlescharte (2455m)
Maps	AV3/3 and AV3/2 (1:25,000)
	FB351 (1:50,000)
	K24 (1:50,000)

The hard stuff is behind you. After an initial short but fairly steep ascent to Schindlescharte, with some aided sections, it is downhill to Leutkircherhutte and on to St Anton. The upper slopes of tussock grass give way to alpine meadows with a sea of alpine flowers in season, then down through dwarf conifers and into forest before arriving at the St Anton suburb of Nasserein.

Leave **Kaiserjochhaus** (sp Leutkircherhutte) on a path zigzagging W up a grassy ridge over Kaiserkopf, with a steep drop into a bowl R. Continue ascending across grassy slopes towards Schindlescharte notch, to a junction where a path L leads to the summit of Schindlekopf (40mins).

See map on p177

Continue a short distance to the top of the col (2455m), then follow an undulating traverse below the screes of Stanskogel R. At Gaisswasen you reach a path junction R, where a path zigzags up to Stanskogel summit (35mins).

Bear L, rounding the shoulder of Hirschpleis, where views open out of St Anton and the intensively developed

Leutkircherhutte, with St Anton in the valley below

From Almajurjoch col, top left, the path descends across meadows and through forest to St Anton

ski slopes on the mountainsides beyond Almajurjoch, and descend to a path junction R (25mins).

From here, an eroded path drops down to **Leutkircherhutte** (2261m) (DAV, 50 beds 8b/42d, meals/refreshments, late June to mid-September, tel 0664 985 7849) (20mins).

From Leutkircherhutte a stony path (sp St Anton) descends SE then S and finally SW across grassy meadows. Pass a small chalet with a balcony L, and continue straight ahead at a path junction. Reaching the tree line, pass through dwarf conifers and cross a 4wd track. Continue down through bigger trees. At an unmarked path junction, turn R cutting through a small ridge to drop down to a good quality 4wd track just before a sharp hairpin bend (50mins).

Turn R and follow the track as it zigzags down into Schongraben valley. Some of the bends can be shortened by obvious cut-offs. Pass a 4wd track L, and continue around a bend R to reach a bridge R, just before passing under power cables (30mins).

St Anton town centre

Cross the bridge and fork L along the opposite bank on a track that soon becomes surfaced. Passing the end of the *rodelbahn*, where toboggans can be hired in winter, you reach the St Anton suburb of **Nasserein**. Continue on this road round a series of bends L and R, passing numerous apartments and ski chalets, to reach the base station of Nasserein chairlift (20mins).

Further on, the road reaches Dorfstrasse, the main street through **St Anton**. Turn R and follow this street for 1.1km, passing through the town centre to reach the tourist office L (1284m) (20mins).

For details of onward transport from St Anton, see 'Getting there' in the Introduction.

APPENDIX A
Distances and timings

Timings are based on an average walker carrying a moderate pack in good weather conditions and walking each stage without stopping. You can plan your own schedule but always remember to allow ample time to reach each night's accommodation. See Appendix B for suggested schedules and accommodation to walk the Adlerweg in 15 and 21 days.

Section 1: Kaisergebirge (Stages 1–3)

	Distance	Time
St Johann		
Rummlerhof	4.1km	50mins
Diebshofen	3km	1hr 30mins
Schleierwasserfall	0.8km	30mins
Obere Regalm	2.3km	1hr
Baumgartenkopf	1.1km	45mins
Gaudeamushutte	1.4km	40mins
Ellmau stein kreis	1.9km	40mins

	Distance	Time
Wilder Kaiser Steig	1.2km	40mins
Kaiser Hochalm	4.2km	1hr 30mins
Steiner Hochalm	1.7km	45mins
Hintersteinersee	2.1km	1hr
Walleralm	2.9km	1hr 10mins
Hochegg	1.5km	45mins
Kaindlhutte	1.1km	20mins
Brentenjoch chairlift	3.5km	1hr

Section 2: Brandenberger Alpen and Rofangebirge (Stages 4–7 and U6–U7)

	Distance	Time	Distance	Time
Langkampfen bhf				
Unterlangkampfen	1.1km	15mins		
Hohlensteinhaus	3km	1hr 40mins		
Koglhorndl	1.8km	1hr 10mins		
Hundsalmjoch	1.9km	1hr 20mins		
Daxerkreuz	1.2km	30mins		
Buchackeralm	1.2km	20mins		
Holzerhutte	4.8km	1hr 15mins		
Kaiserklamm	6.5km	1hr 35mins		
Kaiserhaus	0.4km	10mins		
Pinegg	2.4km	35mins		

Stages 6–7	Distance	Time
Gang	4.4km	1hr 10mins
Steinberg am Rofan	5.2km	1hr 20mins
Enterhof	3km	50mins
Schauertalalm	6.1km	2hrs 5mins
Schauertalsattel	1.2km	1hr 20mins
Marchgatterl	1.4km	45mins
Schaftsteigsattel	1.3km	45mins
Mauritzalm	3.8km	1hr 35mins

Stages U6–U7	Distance	Time
Pinegg	2.4km	35mins
Aschau	2.2km	45mins
Brantl	3.2km	1hr 10mins
Eilalm	2.5km	55mins
Anderl	1.7km	40mins
Hochleger	1.5km	35mins
Zireinersee	2.6km	1hr 20mins
Bayreutherhutte	2.1km	1hr 10mins
Sonnwendbichlalm	1.9km	40mins
Schermsteinalm	3.4km	1hr
Krahnsattel	1.4km	40mins
Mauritzalm	2.2km	50mins

Section 3: Karwendelgebirge (Stages 8–12 and U9–U11)

	Distance	Time
Maurach		
Seespitz	1.8km	25mins
Pertisau	3.7km	50mins
Falzthurnalm	3.5km	45mins
Gramaialm	3.7km	1hr
Lamsenjochhutte	4.3km	2hrs
Stages 9–11		
Lamsenjochhutte		
Binsalm Niederleger	2.6km	1hr 15mins
Engalm	2.3km	50mins
Hohljoch	3.1km	1hr 15mins
Falkenhutte	2.8km	1hr 10mins
von Barth monument	4.7km	1hr 45mins
Grasslegerbichl	2.5km	1hr

	Distance	Time
Stages U9–U11		
Lamsenjochhutte		
Stallenhutte	4km	1hr 15mins
Barenrast	3.8km	55mins
Karwendelrast	5.1km	1hr 20mins
Bergblick	2.4km	1hr 15mins
Ganalm	4.8km	1hr 35mins
Walderalm	4.1km	1hr 40mins

	Distance	Time
Karwendelhaus	1.7km	30mins
Schlauchkarsattel	3km	2hrs 15mins
Hinterautal	5km	2hrs 40mins
Kastenalm	0.8km	20mins
Hallerangerhaus	4.9km	1hr 50mins
Lafatscherjoch	2.1km	1hr
Stempeljoch	3.4km	2hrs
Pfeishutte	1.9km	30mins
Stage 12		
Pfeishutte		
Mannlscharte	2.3km	50mins
Hafelekarhaus	3.1km	1hr 10mins

	Distance	Time
Hinterhornalm	1.6km	20mins
Walderbrucke	5.3km	1hr 40mins
St Magdalena	3.6km	1hr 20mins
Herrenhauser	1.7km	30mins
Stempeljoch	3.6km	1hr 40mins
Pfeishutte	1.9km	30mins

Section 4 Innsbruck and Patscherkofel (Stages 12a, 13 and 14)

	Distance	Time
Innsbruck Congresshaus		
Bergisel	3.1km	55mins
Patscherkofelhaus		
Boscheben	2.2km	45mins
Tulfeinalm	5.1km	1hr 45mins
Hochzirl bhf		
Solenalm	4.8km	2hrs
Solsteinhaus	1.7km	45mins

Section 5 Wettersteingebirge and Miemingergebirge (Stages 15–17)

	Distance	Time
Solsteinhaus		
Eppzirlerscharte	1.6km	1hr 10mins
Eppzirleralm	2.6km	1hr
Giessenbach	6.6km	1hr 35mins
Hoher sattel	3.2km	1hr 30mins
Leutasch Arn	2.8km	45mins
Weidach	1.4km	20mins
Klamm	3.7km	55mins
Gaistalalm	6.6km	1hr 45mins
Tilfiussalm	0.9km	15mins
Igelsee	5.4km	1hr 25mins
Ehrwalder Alm	2.5km	40mins
Ehrwald	2.2km	1hr 10mins
Lermoos	3.5km	55mins
Grubigalm		
Fernpass	4.4km	1hr 25mins
Schloss Fernstein castle	3.3km	55mins

Section 6 Lechtal and Valluga (Stages 18–23 and U22)

	Distance	Time		Distance	Time
Schloss Fernstein castle					
Tegestal	2.3km	30mins			
Hintere Tarrentonalm	7.8km	2hrs			
Hinterbergjoch	4.1km	2hrs 15mins			
Kromsattel	0.8km	40mins			
Anhalterhutte	1km	20mins			
Bschlabs	8.5km	2hrs 30mins			
Ort der Stille	1.6km	30mins			
Haselgehr	12.3km	3hrs			
Elbigenalp	5.5km	1hr 15mins			
Bach	3.7km	50mins			
Holzgau	5.3km	1hr 15mins			
Steeg	5km	1hr 10mins			

Stages 21–23

	Distance	Time
Steeg		
Prenten	2.1km	1hr 45mins
Schonegg	7.2km	2hrs 30mins
Furmesgumpalpe	2.5km	1hr
Stuttgarterhutte	2km	1hr
Pazielfernerscharte	3.7km	1hr 55mins
Vallugagrat	0.2km	25mins
Ulmerhutte	2.3km	55mins
St Anton bhf	6.4km	2hrs

Stage U22

	Distance	Time
Steeg		
Kaisers	4km	1hr 45mins
Bodenalpe	5.3km	1hr 15mins
Leutkircherhutte	3.5km	2hrs 30mins
Nasserein	5.3km	1hr 40mins
St Anton bhf	1.1km	20mins

Section 7 Lechtaler Alpen Hohenweg (Stages A17–A24)

	Distance	Time
Schloss Fernstein castle		
Loreahutte	4.1km	2hrs 30mins
Loreascharte	1.3km	50mins
Heimbachtal/Tegestal	4.1km	2hrs 10mins
Hintere Tarrentonalm	4.6km	1hr
Hinterbergjoch	4.1km	2hrs 15mins
Kromsattel	0.8km	40mins
Anhalterhutte	1km	20mins
Hahntennjoch	2.7km	1hr
Pfafflar	2.8km	45mins
Boden	1.4km	30mins
Hanauerhutte	4.9km	2hrs
West Dremelscharte	2.1km	1hr 40mins
Steinseehutte	1.3km	50mins

	Distance	Time
Mittelkopf col	1.7km	1hr
Rosskarscharte	1.2km	45mins
Gebaudjochl	2.6km	1hr 30mins
Wurttembergerhaus	1.1km	30mins
Grossbergspitze	2.2km	1hr 50mins
Seescharte	2.5km	1hr 55mins
Memmingerhutte	2km	1hr 15mins
Parseiertal	3km	1hr 20mins
Schafgufel	1.5km	50mins
Griesslscharte	1.9km	2hrs
Winterjochl	0.9km	40mins
Kopfscharte	1km	40mins
Ansbacherhutte	1.3km	30mins
Flarschjoch	1.1km	25mins

	Distance	Time
Alperschonjoch	1.4km	30mins
Hinterseejochl	2.9km	1hr 35mins
Kridlonscharte	1.2km	40mins
Kaiserjochhaus	1.7km	50mins
Schindlekopf	1.1km	40mins
Leutkircherhutte	3.1km	1hr 20mins
Nasserein	5.3km	1hr 40mins
St Anton	1.1km	20mins

Maypole in St Johann Hauptplatz with Wilderkaiser behind (Stage 1)

APPENDIX B

Suggested 15-day and 21-day schedules

15 day schedule

Day	Overnight	Distance	Time
1	Riedlhutte	16km	6hrs 15mins
2	Kufstein	18km	7hrs 15mins
3	Kaiserhaus	22km	8hrs 15mins
4	Mauritzalm(*)	22km	8hrs 45mins
5	Lamsenjochhutte	17km	5hrs
6	Karwendelhaus	20km	7hrs 45mins
7	Hallerangerhaus	14km	7hrs
8	Innsbruck	13km	5hrs 30mins
9	Solsteinhaus	17km	6hrs 15mins

21 day schedule

Overnight	Distance	Time
Gaudeamushutte	13km	5hrs 15mins
Hintersteinersee	11km	4hrs 45mins
Kufstein	9km	3hrs 15mins
Buchackeralm	10km	5hrs 15mins
Steinberg	24km	6hrs 15mins
Mauritzalm	17km	7hrs 30mins
Lamsenjochhutte	17km	5hrs
Falkenhutte	11km	4hrs 30mins
Karwendelhaus	9km	3hrs 15mins

(*) To get from Kaiserhaus to Mauritzalm on day four, follow Stage U6 from Kaiserhaus to Zireinersee and then take Stage 7 from there to Mauritzalm.

	21 day schedule		
	Overnight	Distance	Time
	Hallerangerhaus	14km	7hrs
	Innsbruck	13km	5hrs 30mins
	Innsbruck	10km	3hrs 30mins
	Solsteinhaus	7km	2hrs 45mins
	Weidach	18km	6hrs 15mins
	Ehrwald	21km	6hrs 15mins
	Schloss Fernstein castle	11km	3hrs 15mins
	Anhalterhutte	16km	5hrs 45mins
	Haselgehr	22km	6hrs
	Steeg	20km	4hrs 30mins
	Stuttgarterhutte	14km	5hrs
	St Anton bhf	13km	5hrs 15mins

	15 day schedule		
Day	Overnight	Distance	Time
10	Weidach	18km	6hrs 15mins
11	Lermoos	25km	7hrs
12	Anhalterhutte	24km	8hrs
13	Elbigenalp	28km	7hrs 15mins
14	Stuttgarterhutte	28km	8hrs 15mins
15	**St Anton bhf**	13km	5hrs 15mins
16			
17			
18			
19			
20			
21			

The Adlerweg enters St Anton by way of Muhltobelweg, a boarded walkway through Steissbachklamm gorge (Stage 23)

APPENDIX C
Tourist offices

St Johann
Poststrasse 2, St Johann 6380
Tel 5352 633350
Stages 1 and 2

Wilderkaiser
Dorf 84, Soll 6306
Tel 5333 5216
Stages 2 and 3

Kufstein
Unt Stadtplatz 8, Kufstein 6330
Tel 5372 62207
Stages 3 and 4

Worgl
Bahnhofstrasse 4a, Worgl 6300
Tel 5332 76007
Stages 4 and 5

Kramsach
Zentrum 1, Kramsach 6233
Tel 5336 600600
Stages 5, 6, U6 and U7

Achensee
Rathaus 387, Achenkirk 6215
Tel 5246 5300
Stages 6, 7, U7 and 8

Maurach
Hnr 82, Maurach, 6212
Tel 5243 53550
Stages 7 and 8

Pertisau
Hnr55d, Pertisau, 6213
Tel 5243 43070
Stage 8

Schwaz
Franz Josef str 2, Schwaz 6130
Tel 5242 63240
Stages 8, 9, 10, U9 and U10

Seefeld
Klosterstrasse 43, Seefeld 6100
Tel 508 800
Stages 10, 11, 15 and 16

Hall in Tirol
Wallpachgasse 5, Hall-i-T 6060
Tel 5223 455440
Stages 12, 13, U10 and U11

Innsbruck
Burggraben 3, Innsbruck 6020
Tel 512 59850
Stages 12, 12a, 13 and 14

Igls
Hilberstasse 15, Igls 6080
Tel 512 377101
Stage 13

Tulfes
Schmalzgasse 27, Tulfes 6075
Tel 5223 78324
Stage 13

Leutasch
Weidach 320, Leutasch 6105
Tel 508 8010
Stage 15 and 16

Ehrwald
Am Rettensee 1, Ehrwald 6632
Tel 5673 20000
Stages 16 and 17

Lermoos
Unterdorf 15, Lermoos 6631
Tel 5673 20000300
Stage 17

Fernpass
Obsteig 6416
Tel 5264 8106
Stages 17, 18 and A17

Imst
Johannesplatz 4, Imst 6460
Tel 5412 69100
Stages 18, 19 and A19

Elbigenalp
Nr 55b, Elbigenalp, 6652
Tel 5634 5315
Stages 19, 20, 21, 22 and A21

Holzgau
Hnr 45, Holzgau 6654
Tel 5633 5356
Stage 20

Steeg
Aqua Nova, Steeg 6655
Tel 5633 5308
Stages 20, 21, 22 and U22

St Anton
Dorfstrasse 8, St Anton 6580
Tel 5446 2269
Stages 22, 23, U22 and A24

Landeck
Malserstrasse 10, Landeck 6500
Tel 5442 65600
Stages A20, A21, A22 and A23

APPENDIX D
Useful contacts

Austrian Alpine Club (UK)
12a North St
Wareham
Dorset BH20 4AG
01929 556 870
aaac.office@aacuk.org.uk
www.aacuk.org.uk

Oesterreichischer Alpenverein
Olympiastrasse 37
Innsbruck 6020, Austria
+43(0)512 59547
office@alpenverein.at
www.alpenverein.at

Stanfords
12/14 Long Acre
Covent Garden
London WC2E 9LP
0207 836 1321
sales@stanfords.co.uk
www.stanfords.co.uk

The Map Shop
15 High St
Upton upon Severn
Worcester WR8 0HJ
0800 085 40 80 or 01684 593146
themapshop@btinternet.com
www.themapshop.co.uk

Freytag and Berndt
Brunner Strasse 69
Wien 1230, Austria
+43(0)1 869 9090 0
office@freytagberndt.com
www.freytagberndt.com

Kompass Karten
Kaplanstrasse 2
Rum 6063, Austria
+43(0)512 265561 0
info@kompass.at
www.kompass.at

Tirol Tourist Information
Maria Theresien Strasse 55
Innsbruck 6010, Austria
+43(0)512 7272 0
info@tirol.at
www.tirol.at
www.adlerweg.tirol.at

OBB (Austrian Railways)
+43(0)51717
www.oebb.at

Deutsche Bahn (DB)
0871 880 8066 (UK)
+49(0)180 5996633
www.bahn.de

Rail Europe
0844 848 4064 (UK)
www.raileurope.co.uk

Bergwetter Osterreich
www.wetter.orf.at/bwx

The forestry road above Vomper Loch canyon is frequently blocked by washouts like this one at Gannerklamm (Stage U10)

The Adlerweg follows Via Claudia Augusta Roman road downhill through Schloss Fernstein castle (Stage 17)

APPENDIX E
Glossary of German geographic terms

German	English	German	English
Ache	river	Karrenweg	bridleway
Alm	mountain pasture	Kette	(mountain) range
alt	old	Klamm	gorge
Aussichtspunkt	viewpoint	Klettersteig	(aided) climbing trail
Autobahn	motorway	Kopf	head/hilltop
Bach	stream/brook	(weg)Kreuz	(wayside) cross
(eisen)bahn	railway	Lande	region
Bahnhof	railway station	Langlauf	cross country ski
Berg	hill/mountain	Mautstrasse	toll road
Bichl	hill	neu	new
Boden	land/bottom/floor	nieder	low/lower
Bruck	bridge	obere	upper
Denkmal	monument	Pfarr	parish
Dorf	village	Quelle	spring
Fahrweg	dirt road	Radweg	cycleway
Friedhof	cemetery	rot	red
Fussweg	footpath	Sattel	saddle/ridge
Gasse	lane	Schloss	castle
Gebirge	mountain range	schwarz	black
Gemeinde	local district	See	lake
Gipfel	summit	Seilbahn	cablecar
Gletscher	glacier	Sender	communications mast
Grenze	boundary	Sessellift	chairlift
haupt	main/chief	Spitze	peak
Haus	house/inn	Stadt	town
hinter	behind/after	Steig	trail
hoch	high	Steinbruch	quarry
hohen	height	Strasse	street
Hohenlinien	contour lines	Tal	valley
Hohenpunkt	highpoint	vorder	front/near
Hohle	cave	Wald	wood/forest
Hutte	hut/cottage/refuge	Waldgrenze	tree line
Jagd hutte	hunting hut	Wasserfall	waterfall
Jausenhutte	barn/feeding place	Weg	way
Joch	col	weiss	white

STAMPS

STAMPS

STAMPS

STAMPS

LISTING OF CICERONE GUIDES

BRITISH ISLES CHALLENGES, COLLECTIONS AND ACTIVITIES

The End to End Trail
The Mountains of England and Wales
1 Wales & 2 England
The National Trails
The Relative Hills of Britain
The Ridges of England, Wales and Ireland
The UK Trailwalker's Handbook
The UK's County Tops
Three Peaks, Ten Tors

MOUNTAIN LITERATURE

Unjustifiable Risk?

UK CYCLING

Border Country Cycle Routes
Cycling in the Peak District
Lands End to John O'Groats Cycle Guide
Mountain Biking in the Lake District
Mountain Biking on the South Downs
The C2C Cycle Route
The Lancashire Cycleway

SCOTLAND

Backpacker's Britain
Central and Southern Scottish Highlands
Northern Scotland
Ben Nevis and Glen Coe
North to the Cape
Not the West Highland Way
Scotland's Best Small Mountains
Scotland's Far West
Scotland's Mountain Ridges
Scrambles in Lochaber
The Ayrshire and Arran Coastal Paths
The Border Country
The Great Glen Way
The Isle of Mull
The Isle of Skye
The Pentland Hills: A Walker's Guide

The Southern Upland Way
The Speyside Way
The West Highland Way
Walking in Scotland's Far North
Walking in the Cairngorms
Walking in the Ochils, Campsie Fells and Lomond Hills
Walking in Torridon
Walking Loch Lomond and the Trossachs
Walking on Harris and Lewis
Walking on Jura, Islay and Colonsay
Walking on the Isle of Arran
Walking on the Orkney and Shetland Isles
Walking the Galloway Hills
Walking the Lowther Hills
Walking the Munros
1 Southern, Central and Western Highlands
2 Northern Highlands and the Cairngorms
Winter Climbs Ben Nevis and Glen Coe
Winter Climbs in the Cairngorms
World Mountain Ranges: Scotland

NORTHERN ENGLAND TRAILS

A Northern Coast to Coast Walk
Backpacker's Britain Northern England
Hadrian's Wall Path
The Dales Way
The Pennine Way
The Spirit of Hadrian's Wall

NORTH EAST ENGLAND, YORKSHIRE DALES AND PENNINES

Historic Walks in North Yorkshire
South Pennine Walks
The Cleveland Way and the Yorkshire Wolds Way
The North York Moors

The Reivers Way
The Teesdale Way
The Yorkshire Dales Angler's Guide
The Yorkshire Dales
North and East
South and West
Walking in County Durham
Walking in Northumberland
Walking in the North Pennines
Walks in Dales Country
Walks in the Yorkshire Dales
Walks on the North York Moors – Books 1 & 2

NORTH WEST ENGLAND AND THE ISLE OF MAN

Historic Walks in Cheshire
Isle of Man Coastal Path
The Isle of Man
The Ribble Way
Walking in Cumbria's Eden Valley
Walking in Lancashire
Walking in the Forest of Bowland and Pendle
Walking on the West Pennine Moors
Walks in Lancashire Witch Country
Walks in Ribble Country
Walks in Silverdale and Arnside
Walks in the Forest of Bowland

LAKE DISTRICT

Coniston Copper Mines
Great Mountain Days in the Lake District
Lake District Winter Climbs
Lakeland Fellranger
The Central Fells
The Mid-Western Fells
The Near Eastern Fells
The North-Western Wells
The Southern Fells
The Western Fells
Roads and Tracks of the Lake District

Rocky Rambler's Wild Walks
Scrambles in the Lake District North & South
Short Walks in Lakeland
  1 South Lakeland
  2 North Lakeland
  3 West Lakeland
The Cumbria Coastal Way
The Cumbria Way and the Allerdale Ramble
Tour of the Lake District

DERBYSHIRE, PEAK DISTRICT AND MIDLANDS

High Peak Walks
Scrambles in the Dark Peak
The Star Family Walks
Walking in Derbyshire
White Peak Walks
  The Northern Dales
  The Southern Dales

SOUTHERN ENGLAND

A Walker's Guide to the Isle of Wight
London – The definitive walking guide
Suffolk Coast and Heaths Walks
The Cotswold Way
The North Downs Way
The South Downs Way
The South West Coast Path
The Thames Path
Walking in Berkshire
Walking in Kent
Walking in Sussex
Walking in the Isles of Scilly
Walking in the Thames Valley
Walking on Dartmoor
Walking on Guernsey
Walking in Jersey
Walks in the South Downs National Park

WALES AND WELSH BORDERS

Backpacker's Britain – Wales
Glyndwr's Way
Great Mountain Days in Snowdonia
Hillwalking in Snowdonia

Hillwalking in Wales
  Vols 1 & 2
Offa's Dyke Path
Ridges of Snowdonia
Scrambles in Snowdonia
The Ascent of Snowdon
The Lleyn Peninsula Coastal Path
The Pembrokeshire Coastal Path
The Shropshire Hills
The Wye Valley Walk
Walking in Pembrokeshire
Walking on the Brecon Beacons
Welsh Winter Climbs

INTERNATIONAL CHALLENGES, COLLECTIONS AND ACTIVITIES

Canyoning
Europe's High Points
The Via Francigena (Canterbury to Rome): Part 1

EUROPEAN CYCLING

Cycle Touring in France
Cycle Touring in Ireland
Cycle Touring in Spain
Cycle Touring in Switzerland
Cycling in the French Alps
Cycling the Canal du Midi
Cycling the River Loire
The Danube Cycleway
The Grand Traverse of the Massif Central
The Way of St James

AFRICA

Climbing in the Moroccan Anti-Atlas
Kilimanjaro: A Complete Trekker's Guide
Mountaineering in the Moroccan High Atlas
Trekking in the Atlas Mountains
Walking in the Drakensberg

ALPS – CROSS-BORDER ROUTES

100 Hut Walks in the Alps

Across the Eastern Alps: E5
Alpine Points of View
Alpine Ski Mountaineering
  1 Western Alps
  2 Central and Eastern Alps
Chamonix to Zermatt
Snowshoeing
Tour of Mont Blanc
Tour of Monte Rosa
Tour of the Matterhorn
Trekking in the Alps
Walking in the Alps
Walks and Treks in the Maritime Alps

PYRENEES AND FRANCE/ SPAIN CROSS-BORDER ROUTES

Rock Climbs in The Pyrenees
The GR10 Trail
The Mountains of Andorra
The Pyrenean Haute Route
The Pyrenees
The Way of St James
  France & Spain
Through the Spanish Pyrenees: GR11
Walks and Climbs in the Pyrenees

AUSTRIA

The Adlerweg
Trekking in Austria's Hohe Tauern
Trekking in the Stubai Alps
Trekking in the Zillertal Alps
Walking in Austria

EASTERN EUROPE

The High Tatras
The Mountains of Romania
Walking in Bulgaria's National Parks
Walking in Hungary

FRANCE

Ecrins National Park
GR20: Corsica
Mont Blanc Walks
Mountain Adventures in the Maurienne
The Cathar Way
The GR5 Trail

The Robert Louis Stevenson
   Trail
Tour of the Oisans: The GR54
Tour of the Queyras
Tour of the Vanoise
Trekking in the Vosges and Jura
Vanoise Ski Touring
Walking in Provence
Walking in the Cathar Region
Walking in the Cevennes
Walking in the Dordogne
Walking in the Haute Savoie
   North & South
Walking in the Languedoc
Walking in the Tarentaise and
   Beaufortain Alps
Walking on Corsica

GERMANY

Germany's Romantic Road
Walking in the Bavarian Alps
Walking in the Harz Mountains
Walking the River Rhine Trail

HIMALAYA

Annapurna: A Trekker's Guide
Bhutan
Everest: A Trekker's Guide
Garhwal and Kumaon: A
   Trekker's and Visitor's Guide
Kangchenjunga: A Trekker's
   Guide
Langtang with Gosainkund and
   Helambu: A Trekker's Guide
Manaslu: A Trekker's Guide
The Mount Kailash Trek

IRELAND

Irish Coastal Walks
The Irish Coast to Coast Walk
The Mountains of Ireland

ITALY

Gran Paradiso
Italy's Sibillini National Park
Shorter Walks in the Dolomites
Through the Italian Alps
Trekking in the Apennines
Trekking in the Dolomites
Via Ferratas of the Italian
   Dolomites: Vols 1 & 2
Walking in Abruzzo
Walking in Sardinia

Walking in Sicily
Walking in the Central Italian
   Alps
Walking in the Dolomites
Walking in Tuscany
Walking on the Amalfi Coast

MEDITERRANEAN

Jordan – Walks, Treks, Caves,
   Climbs and Canyons
The Ala Dag
The High Mountains of Crete
The Mountains of Greece
Treks and Climbs in Wadi
   Rum, Jordan
Walking in Malta
Western Crete

NORTH AMERICA

British Columbia
The Grand Canyon
The John Muir Trail
The Pacific Crest Trail

SOUTH AMERICA

Aconcagua and the Southern
   Andes
Hiking and Biking Peru's Inca
   Trails
Torres del Paine

SCANDINAVIA

Trekking in Greenland
Walking in Norway

SLOVENIA, CROATIA AND
MONTENEGRO

The Julian Alps of Slovenia
The Mountains of Montenegro
Trekking in Slovenia
Walking in Croatia

SPAIN AND PORTUGAL

Costa Blanca Walks
   1 West & 2 East
Mountain Walking in Southern
   Catalunya
The Mountains of Central Spain
Trekking through Mallorca
Walking in Madeira
Walking in Mallorca
Walking in the Algarve
Walking in the Canary Islands
   2 East

Walking in the Cordillera
   Cantabrica
Walking in the Sierra Nevada
Walking on La Gomera and
   El Hierro
Walking on La Palma
Walking on Tenerife
Walking the GR7 in Andalucia
Walks and Climbs in the Picos
   de Europa

SWITZERLAND

Alpine Pass Route
Central Switzerland
The Bernese Alps
The Swiss Alps
Tour of the Jungfrau Region
Walking in the Valais
Walking in Ticino
Walks in the Engadine

TECHNIQUES

Geocaching in the UK
Indoor Climbing
Lightweight Camping
Map and Compass
Mountain Weather
Moveable Feasts
Outdoor Photography
Rock Climbing
Sport Climbing
The Book of the Bivvy
The Hillwalker's Guide to
   Mountaineering
The Hillwalker's Manual

MINI GUIDES

Avalanche!
Navigating with a GPS
Navigation
Pocket First Aid and Wilderness
   Medicine
Snow

For full information on all
our guides, and to order
books and eBooks, visit our
website:
www.cicerone.co.uk.

Walking – Trekking – Mountaineering – Climbing – Cycling

Over 40 years, Cicerone have built up an outstanding collection of 300 guides, inspiring all sorts of amazing adventures.

Every guide comes from extensive exploration and research by our expert authors, all with a passion for their subjects. They are frequently praised, endorsed and used by clubs, instructors and outdoor organisations.

All our titles can now be bought as **e-books** and many as iPad and Kindle files and we will continue to make all our guides available for these and many other devices.

Our website shows any **new information** we've received since a book was published. Please do let us know if you find anything has changed, so that we can pass on the latest details. On our **website** you'll also find some great ideas and lots of information, including sample chapters, contents lists, reviews, articles and a photo gallery.

It's easy to keep in touch with what's going on at Cicerone, by getting our monthly **free e-newsletter**, which is full of offers, competitions, up-to-date information and topical articles. You can subscribe on our home page and also follow us on **Facebook** and **Twitter**, as well as our **blog**.

Cicerone – the very best guides for exploring the world.

CICERONE

2 Police Square Milnthorpe Cumbria LA7 7PY
Tel: 015395 62069 info@cicerone.co.uk
www.cicerone.co.uk